Cyra

Martin Crimp was bor[n]
Her Life (1997) established his international reputation.
His other work for theatre includes *When We Have
Sufficiently Tortured Each Other*, *Men Asleep*, *The Rest
Will be Familiar to You from Cinema*, *In the Republic
of Happiness*, *Play House*, *The City*, *Fewer Emergencies*,
Cruel and Tender, *The Country*, *The Treatment*, *Getting
Attention*, *No One Sees the Video*, *Play with Repeats*,
Dealing with Clair and *Definitely the Bahamas*. He is
also the author of three texts, *Into the Little Hill*,
Written on Skin and *Lessons in Love and Violence*, for
operas by George Benjamin. His many translations of
French plays include works by Genet, Ionesco, Koltès,
Marivaux and Molière. *Writing for Nothing*, a collection
of fiction, short plays and texts for opera, was published
by Faber & Faber in 2019.

MARTIN CRIMP

Cyrano de Bergerac

freely adapted from the play by

EDMOND ROSTAND

FABER & FABER

First published in 2019
by Faber and Faber Limited
74–77 Great Russell Street, London WC1B 3DA

Typeset by Country Setting, Kingsdown, Kent CT14 8ES
Printed in England by by CPI Group (UK) Ltd, Croydon CR0 4YY

A CIP record for this book
is available from the British Library

ISBN 978-0-571-36140-3

4 6 8 10 9 7 5

Cyrano de Bergerac in this adaptation was first performed at the Playhouse Theatre, London, on 27 November 2019. The cast, in alphabetical order, was as follows:

Leila Ragueneau Michele Austin
Le Bret Adam Best
Armand / Priest Sam Black
Valvert Nari Blair-Mangat
Jean-Paul Philip Cairns
De Guiche Tom Edden
Christian Eben Figueiredo
Usher Chris Fung
Montfleury Adrian Der Gregorian
Denise Carla Harrison-Hodge
Cyrano James McAvoy
Theatre Owner Seun Shote
Marie-Louise Kiruna Stamell
Lignière Nima Taleghani
Roxane Anita-Joy Uwajeh
Ensemble Vaneeka Dadhria, Mika Johnson,
    Brinsley Terence

All other roles played by members of the company.

Director Jamie Lloyd
Designer Soutra Gilmour
Lighting Design Jon Clark
Sound and Composition Ben and Max Ringham
Casting Director Stuart Burt CDG
Fight Movement Kate Waters
Additional Movement Direction Polly Bennett
Associate Director Rupert Hands
Associate Designer Rachel Wingate

Characters

Roxane

Cyrano

Lignière

Christian

Leila Ragueneau

Le Bret

De Guiche

Alastair

Valvert

Montfleury

Theatre Owner

Usher

Annoying Person

Fencing Referee

Woman Sent by Roxane

Marie-Louise (student)

Armande (student)

Denise (student)

Group of Soldiers

Priest

Audience members and
people who shout from the auditorium

Author's Notes

A slash (/) shows the point of interruption in overlapping dialogue.

A long dash (——) introduces lines to be attributed to audience members, soldiers etc., according to the forces available for a given production.

PRONUNCIATION

Cyrano (Si-ra-no) Stressed on first and sometimes also last syllable.

Christian (Crist-yan) Stressed on final syllable – rhymes with 'man' etc.

Lignière (Lee-nyere) Stressed on final syllable – rhymes with 'where' etc.

Ragueneau (Rag-no) Two equal stresses. Rhymes with 'go' etc.

De Guiche (d' geesh) Rhymes with 'leash' etc.

Madeleine Robin (Ro-ban) Stressed on final syllable – rhymes with 'man' etc.

CYRANO DE BERGERAC

Act One

*Onstage activity as the audience comes in. Perhaps
stagehands are completing a rostrum or some other
installation for Montfleury's play – or working on a
lighting-rig which will later fly up.*

*While this happens, a number of characters drift on,
watch and comment, some holding drinks. Later we will
identify these as fans of the actor Montfleury – or
enemies – critics – and general hangers-on.*

*House lights come down as Lignière propels Christian
on to the stage.*

Lignière So this is our famous theatre –

Christian Amazing.

Lignière And at the moment as you can see we
appear to be playing the part
of people waiting for a play to start.
Ladies, gentlemen – meet Christian.
Christian's like your alpha-male-type ultra-military man
but pretty cool, and will be joining our friend Cyrano's
elite cadets.

—— Congratulations.

Lignière Plus he is new to Paris so let's
not be too cruel, please – I'd like us all to welcome him.

—— Good-looking boy.

Lignière Hands off. Christian is exclusively into women.

—— Too bad.

3

Christian   One woman, actually.

——   Even worse.

—— Bit provincial.

——   Got your tongue round the language?

——   Speak much verse?

Christian Look, I might not come from Paris
      but I work out and I'm pretty fit
  and verse or no verse I'd like to point out right now
      I don't take any shit.

—— Bravo! The man's got attitude.

Lignière The man has indeed got attitude
  cut him some slack give him some latitude
  do not attack him with platitudinous crap
  or he will fight back see what he'll do to us
  this is a man you cannot embarrass
  even a man this new to Paris
  is a man you may not disparage
  look at the man and the way he carries
  himself he will not be abandoned in Paris.
  The Parisian isn't superior
  just everyone else is inferior
  sure it's not bad as a theory. Ah –
  just never mention Algeria.

Christian   Wow.

Lignière   You into words? Do much poetry?

Christian I'm not much of a confident speaker actually.

—— Who's the 'one woman', sweetheart?

Christian   I'm not sure – I'm –

—— Not sure?

Lignière   Someone get me a glass of wine?

4

—— How can you be not sure?

Lignière   Give him a break.
He's seen her but he doesn't know her name.
                    (*To Christian.*) Okay – take
a good look round the auditorium
and point her out –

Wine served to Christian and Lignière.

                    — thank you – my moratorium
on alcohol is fortunately over – hey –
                              Christian – *cincin*!

They clink glasses and scan the auditorium.

Right – let's begin
with the back row . . . hmm – d'you see her? –
there's quite a few hot women, but we must still be a
bit early.

Christian   Who're those weird guys?

Lignière   That's the Académie Française –
they check out all the plays
and kind of sit
in judgement over grammar
              – no foreign words – that kind of shit –
ignore them.

Christian   That attractive girl up there . . .

Lignière Is actually a man. How's it going, Alastair?

—— I'm good thanks!

Lignière   Straight – just likes to cross-dress.

Christian Cross-what?

Lignière   Quite an important artist – special guest.

Christian You mean he . . .?

Lignière Like a persona – kind of cool –
  gender-fluidity? – man – woman – no fixed rule?

Christian Fluidity?

——   Keep up, sweetheart – where've you BEEN?

Lignière He comes from a little village. Don't be too mean.
  They haven't quite made it into the seventeenth century.

Christian Yeah I'm medieval man, essentially.

—— Try and remember: *gender-fluid*.

Lignière The boy's not stupid – he can do it.

Christian Oh God – is that a whole row of students?

Lignière   Sure –
  from the University –
                  what're you looking so frightened for?

Christian Just this intellectual thing is so scary –
  I'm just a soldier – I mean what if SHE
  turns out to be an intellectual too?
  What is this deal with language?
                          I won't know what to do.

—— Poor baby.

Lignière   If you were a student you'd soon find out
  they spend most of their free time
                  fucking each other's brains out –
  Hey! Leila!

Leila   Lignière!

Lignière Leila! Get your ass over here!

  Madame Ragueneau has appeared. They hug.

  Leila – Christian. Christian – Leila.

Leila Good-looking boy.

6

Lignière   Leila is my saviour
she has rescued me from failure
shown me the direction of Arcadia
given me her protection and I say to her
you have given me the writer's toolkit
and / delivered me from –

Leila (*smiles*)   Ease up, Lignière –
                            cut out the saviour bullshit.
(*To Christian.*) I simply teach.
I try to reach
– Christian – out into the community
and I encourage all kinds of spoken word –
                            theatre – poetry –
plus have an interest in literature and cookery.

Lignière Genius in fact.

Leila   Please don't exaggerate –
this young man was my pupil – I simply facilitate –
and when it comes to a real talent like Lignière
beg him please to avoid politics and take care.
You meddle in that satirical political shit –
end up like Cyrano – then you pay for it.

Christian Cyrano?

Leila   You haven't heard?
Cyrano is like all time crazy genius of the spoken word.
Where is he?

——   Not in the house.

Leila   Okay –
but Montfleury is acting in the play?

—— Sure.

Leila And Cyrano has told him no no no
no Montfleury on stage. Personal veto.

—— That's right. For the whole season.

Leila   Then it's clear
to me Cyrano is going to appear.

Christian So this . . . Cyrano –

Lignière   Le Bret! Le Bret!
Le Bret is his closest colleague.

Le Bret   What?

Lignière Tell him about Cyrano.

Le Bret   Ha!
Madman. Soldier. Writer. Blunt. Bizarre.
Masterful swordsman. Courageous. Honest.
Wild and outspoken. Angry idealist.
What d'you reckon, Leila? – am I close?

Leila Kind of. (*To Christian.*) Mister le Bret
                    is leaving out the nose.

Christian The what?

Lignière   Oh oh oh oh – don't even go there.

Leila But his nose is what defines him, Lignière.
(*To Christian.*) Young man, the enormity
of his nose is a deformity
which those who've never seen it
can hardly imagine. Don't laugh, please, I mean it.
They say when he came through his mother's vagina
the nose poked out first as a painful reminder
of all the agony to come. Poor girl nearly died
of shock and needed to be anaesthetised.
When you first see it you say to yourself NO! –
That is a party-trick – take it off, Cyrano –
you expect him to reach up and somehow unscrew it.
But the damage is done: he can never undo it.

Christian She's joking.

Leila   Don't believe what I said?

8

It's God's truth.

Lignière   Yeah and refer to it and you're dead.

A disturbance high up in the audience. Some of the men on stage look up.

—— She's quite something – look at that –
                                    hot – but refined –

—— Fancy your chances?

——   Do you?

——   Wouldn't mind.

Christian (*follows their gaze*)   Lignière. That's her.

Lignière The lady?

Christian   Yes.

Lignière   Where?

Christian   At the back.

Lignière   Keep calm, man – don't stare.

He takes a look.

Okay . . . that is Madeleine – Madeleine Robin –
icon of totally transcendent beauty – aka Roxane.

Christian And?

Lignière   And she's a student – into poetry –

Christian Shit.

Lignière   – super-bright girl – got into the University –

Christian Fuck.

Lignière   – despite being a woman.
She's totally cool, man – plus she is Cyrano's cousin.

Christian There's a man – who's that?

Lignière   Now that is de Guiche –
  he's like a member of Cardinal Richelieu's
                                    very own thought-police –
  impressive soldier – married man –
                                    to Richelieu's own niece –
  and violent opponent of free-speech.
  Class –
  but check out that hand of his touching her ass.
  (*Restraining Christian.*) – Hey, hey, hey –
  Now de Guiche is forcing her to marry
                                    the other guy –
  that one there –
  the name's Valvert –
  steady – steady – try not to stare –
  and the reason is is his long-term plan
  is that once she's safely married he can
  make 'conjugal visits'. She hates him. But the fact
  is she's a woman – he's got the power
                                    and she's trapped.
  I've written about this shit –
  anonymously, so I'm chilled –
  but if the fucker knew who wrote it he would
                                    have me killed.
  So that's your lady.

Christian (*of de Guiche*) Bastard.

Lignière   What can we do?
  Keep out of it, my friend, or he will kill you too.
  Christian! Christian!

Christian   What?

Lignière   She's giving you the eye.
  She is a goddess! (*Pause.*) Sorry, man – I –

Christian Lignière?

10

Lignière I'm out of here – that Guiche guy scares me –
I think

I need some air and get myself a drink.

Christian Lignière – please –

But Lignière goes, as Le Bret returns.
At the same time, de Guiche leaves Roxane and
starts to make his way down to the stage with Valvert.

Leila Well? Did you find him?

Le Bret
Been round the whole theatre – no – no sign of him.

Leila Cyrano's here. I'd take a bet on it.

—— (*Shouts.*) We want the play – come on – get on with it!

Leila Mister de Guiche – an unexpected delight.

De Guiche Madame Ragueneau – not baking in
your charming little bookshop then tonight?

Leila Decided to come out and watch a play.

De Guiche Well well – you don't say –
if you could just move a little out of the way –
come on, Valvert – we'll sit on stage –
apparently this so-called play was all the rage
in London about forty years ago –
what is the play called, Madame Ragueneau?

Leila *Hamlet.*

De Guiche *Hamlet.* How very quaint. Some tragedy –
and the whole thing translated into modern French
and performed by the excellent Montfleury.

Valvert Talented man.

De Guiche Yes and much less of a ham
than they say.

An Usher has appeared.

Usher   Sir?

De Guiche   Well what the fuck is it?

Usher Excuse me, sir – can I see your ticket?

De Guiche Ticket? Ticket? D'you know who I am?

——— (*Shouts*) Come on! – start the play! –

it should've begun!

De Guiche I don't buy tickets – I'm the theatre's guest.

Valvert Outrageous.

———   (*Shouts.*) Start the play!

De Guiche   I actually invest
in this theatre. D'you know who my uncle is?
Richelieu. Who is here tonight. You're taking the piss.

Usher Just you do need a ticket.

——— (*Shouts.*) Start the play and stop talking!

Valvert (*waving the Usher away*) That's it, my sweet –
off you go – back to your little tip-up seat.

*As the Usher withdraws, the onstage audience settles,
the lights change – and Montfleury appears.*

Silence.

Montfleury Amlet
by Guillaume Shakespeare
in a nouvelle version
by myself.

Lights change again to tight focus on the actor's face.

Silence.

'Oh what a rogue and peasant slave am I!
Is it not monstrous that this player here –'

He produces, perhaps, a glove-puppet.

'– but in a fiction, in a dream of passion
could force his soul so to his own conceit
that like a piece of well-cooked tender turkey-meat
hot juices leak from these two apertures
that we call eyes? What's Ecuba to him
or he to Ophelia? Who is this mobled queen
that he should weep for her?
                    What would he do / had he – ?'

Cyrano (*unseen*) I'd get off stage now if I were you.

—— Be quiet.

——   Shut up.

——   Mobled queen?

                              Mobled queen is good.

—— Go for it, Montfleury!

Montfleury recovers his composure and resumes.

Montfleury   'What's Ecuba to him
or he to Ophelia? Who is this mobled queen
that he should weep for her? What would he do
had he my motive and my cue
for passion? To be or not to be –'

Cyrano (*unseen*)
I said get off that stage now, Montfleury –

Montfleury
'– to be a puppet on the puppet-stage of history –
perchance to dream – what do I mean? –
                              I mean to dream of how
that nymph, the fair Ophelia –'

Cyrano   I said stop now!

Cyrano invades the stage. Catcalls etc.

I have forbidden you to act here,
Montfleury. Now disappear.

Montfleury These gentlemen are my sponsors.

Cyrano   Oh?

Montfleury
They've asked me for my Amlet and I refuse to go.

Cyrano Uh-huh – these gentlemen – is that so?

—— (*chant*) Montfleury! Montfleury! Montfleury!

Cyrano scrutinises Montfleury's supporters. Pause.

Cyrano Mobled queen.

——   We like it.

——   Mobled queen is good.

Cyrano The play is over – it is over – is that understood?

Le Bret Cyrano, please, you don't have the right / to –

Cyrano
The play is over and I would be very happy to fight to
make my point. Well?

——   We may not understand it
but we like his acting and we want Amlet.

A chant begins from Montfleury's fans:

—— AM-LET! AM-LET! AM-LET! AM-LET!

*Cyrano draws his sword – this may be enough – or
maybe he holds it to Montfleury's throat.
    The chanting dies down. Silence.*

Cyrano This is a bad actor. He's wrecked
my evening and he's massacred the text.

Catcalls.

And if any one of you believes that 'not to be'
the case you are welcome to defend him in a duel –
                with me.
Any takers? No one? Come on. Don't be shy.
There must be one of you out there who wants to die.

Pause.

Le Bret (*sotto*) Cyrano . . .

Cyrano   I'm counting to three
and on the third stroke you will vanish, Montfleury.

Montfleury Excuse me?

Cyrano   One.

——   Bullshit.

——   Vanish? How?

Cyrano Two.

Montfleury You're so full of crap.

Cyrano   Oh am I now?

—— Come on, Cyrano – do it!

——   This I must see.

—— He's bluffing.

——   It's just Gascon bullshit.

Cyrano   Three.

Montfleury disappears.
   Wild applause and catcalls from the crowd.
   The Theatre Owner steps forward and shakes
Cyrano's hand.

Theatre Owner Good evening, Monsieur de Bergerac.
Congratulations. Your novelty act
adds lustre to my theatre. But Montfleury

is good box-office – well, as you can see –
and I'm just curious why you're so anti.

Cyrano I dislike arrogance. 'His' Hamlet –
credit to the writer damn it! –
plus there could be nothing worse than
his garbled dipshit incoherent version.

Theatre Owner Dislike arrogance. Hmm.

He savours the irony of this . . .

                                You've no other reason
for banning him from my theatre then
                        for an entire season?

Cyrano Arrogance is enough.

Theatre Owner   Arrogance is enough. Indeed.
Arrogance can be destructive – agreed, agreed.
But Montfleury, Monsieur de Bergerac,
brings in the punters. You've stopped the show.
                        Now I must pay them back.

Cyrano Sure. Here's your money. Take it.
                        You'll find it more than meets
the shortfall from your lost box-office receipts.

Theatre Owner Well – if what he says is right
I ought to get him here to cancel every night.

Laughter. The Owner starts counting the money.

Le Bret (*sotto*) Cyrano – stop this – you're going to make it
worse.

Theatre Owner (*genuine shock*)
            But this is far too much money.

Cyrano   Take it.

—— That's quite some gesture.

——   Must be several thousand.

Cyrano shrugs. An annoying person butts in.

Annoying Person But the real question is: how will a little man like you survive? Who will protect you? Montfleury's got high-up friends. He will expect them to exact revenge. Like Hamlet. You should check out the politics before you stick your neck out.

Cyrano My neck?

Annoying Person Yes.

Pause.

Cyrano So why are you looking at my nose?

Annoying Person I'm not.

Cyrano Draws attention, does it?

Annoying Person No way.

Cyrano Too big? Is it grotesque? Just say.

Annoying Person I'm not.

Cyrano Not looking?

Annoying Person No.

Cyrano Why's that?

Annoying Person Just not.

Cyrano Too long? Is it too thin? too fat? Come on. Not looking?

Annoying Person No!

Cyrano Then tell me why. Is it obscene? Is it too shocking?

Annoying Person I . . .

Cyrano Yes?

Annoying Person I'd say it's absolutely normal –

Cyrano Normal?

Annoying Person Yes. If anything . . . quite small.

Cyrano Quite small? What? I take that as a personal
  insult. Small?

Annoying Person Yes.

Cyrano   But my nose is *huge* –
  it's huge, my friend – this 'I'm not looking' subterfuge
  is crass. My nose is out – it's out and proud –
  it's out there – it's full-volume – loud –
  it blasts the world – thrusts and attacks –
  my nose is permanently – yes? yes? –
                      hear it? – set to max –
  and at the same time is the sign
  of probity – wit – magnificence – sure I'm
  a little crazy, but this organ represents
  courage – courtesy to others –

                        genuine independence –
  things you will never have. You're full of shit:
  you cannot grow my nose, nor can you diminish it.

De Guiche This is pathetic – what courtesy? –
                      the man's totally obsessed
  by his own self-image.

Valvert   Yes, we are not impressed.

Cyrano Oh?

De Guiche   Give him both barrels, Valvert.

Cyrano (*on the alert*)   Valvert?

De Guiche
  Valvert's a great wit. Come on, man – don't spare
  the pompous bastard – he sees he's
  gone too far – tear him to pieces.

Valvert – who's not too keen on the job he's been given – nevertheless steps up to Cyrano, and appraises him, before speaking.

Valvert You claim that your nose – sir –
                        puts us on the wrong side
But I say your nose – sir –
                        is a bit on the long side.

*Sparse applause from de Guiche's team.
    Pause.*

Cyrano Is that it?

De Guiche   Both barrels, Valvert.

Valvert That was both barrels.

Cyrano   Yes, be fair
to the poor man. He has tried –
but his intelligence is limited and his wit,
    as we can all see, somewhat circumscribed.
But look, he's just a poor little rich boy arsehole
brought up in Mummy and Daddy's family castle –

Valvert Excuse me?

Cyrano   – where only the housekeeper and cooks
took any interest in things like books.
Yes, you'd think it would be easy to insult me
given the nature of my deformity
but it takes some literary imagination, actually –
no no don't run away –

                        stay here, Valvert, stay a while –
while I take you through some possible variants
                        of the insult style.
Blunt, for example – blunt goes
'Why not take a chopper and chop off your nose' –
then there's tactful: tactful's more like 'Oh yes – I see –
but doesn't it interfere with one's ability
                        to drink one's tea?'

Or if style points you in a sexual direction
you might like to refer, Valvert, to my nasal erection
or if that's too tasteless how about carrot? –
rhinoceros horn? – coat-hook? – yes? –

                                        perch for a parrot?
Use whatever image comes to mind:
cattle-prod – truncheon. Or be more refined –
be Homeric – say 'So noble! Such force!
As hollow and vast as the Trojan Horse!'
You should treat my nose as a literary test:
try out ideas – see what works best.
Picture for example what it's like when it bleeds:
how a blood-red tide floods out then recedes
as its cavernous nostrils are cleansed by what? –
 yes a syrup-like stream of soft grey snot.
Or creatively use the question-mark:
'What's its name?' 'Can it talk?' 'Does it glow in the
    dark?'
'Is it stiff?' 'Will it bend?' 'Might it shrink?'

                                        'Has it grown?'
'Is it ever allowed to go out on its own?'
'Can it think for itself?' 'Might it reproduce?'
'Oh my God don't tell me it's suffered childhood abuse!'
D'you see what I'm saying? – I'm bored, I'm tired
of insults like yours that are

                            one-dimensional and uninspired.
'Your nose is a rock, it's a mountain-range:
sheer – Olympian – dangerous – strange –
and upon its granite storm-swept peak
heroes still tread and the Greek gods still speak.' –
Yes that's the kind of thing you might've said
if you'd one active brain-cell in your head.

Approaching Valvert . . .

But look at you – tongue-tied – hopeless – look –
never thinks about words – never reads a book –

got those dull little eyes you always find
in a person cursed with a blanked-out mind.
And yes I do mean to offend. That is my intention.
I despise the banal. I admire invention
however outrageous or violent in tone –
provided of course the invention's my own –

De Guiche Valvert – no!

Valvert slaps Cyrano. Pause.

Valvert (*seething*)   Scum of pretension.
Filth off the street too disgusting to mention.
Shit-for-brains poet. Mindless talentless hack.

Cyrano (*offers hand*) And I – am Cyrano de Bergerac.

Laughter.

De Guiche (*sotto*) Back down, Valvert.

Cyrano   Oh? Too late now.
He's made his challenge. So listen, my friend, how
shall we do this? Pistols at dawn?
Or are you more of a rapiers drawn
kind of man like me?

De Guiche (*sotto*)   Don't. He'll kill you. This is / insane.

Valvert Swords. I will cut you into tiny pieces.

Cyrano Excellent.

Pause.

          So why don't I give you a little rapier lesson
and at the same time make up a poem.

Valvert Poem?

Cyrano   Poem – yes – quite strict metrically
and with three clear stanzas – d'you follow me?

Valvert Stanzas – whatever – I am completely bored with this –

Cyrano   And whoever draws first blood wins. Agreed? Oh – and one other thing –

Valvert What? This is just pure delaying / tactics –

Cyrano I will improvise the poem now in real time and not draw blood till I get to the final rhyme.

Slight pause. Cyrano closes his eyes and thinks for a moment.

I warned this man his perfumed skin.

Valvert Excuse me?

Cyrano   That's the title. Okay, shall we begin? Please can we clear everyone out of the way.

The crowd makes a space. Someone steps forward to referee.

Referee En garde. – Prêts? – Allez.
[*Take up positions. Ready? Begin.*]

Cyrano I take up my position thus
see how the metal gleams
cutting the space in front of me:
sixte, quarte, octave, septime.

They fight. Valvert holds his own.

Beat! Coule! Balestra! Oh I see –
you're pretty good at it! –

Referee Halte! [*Stop.*]

No result. They separate.

Two stanzas more and I will land
a palpable hit.

Valvert Forget the poetry bollocks – let's just play.

Cyrano Verse two.

Valvert Whatever.

Referee En garde. – Prêts? – Allez.

They fight.

Cyrano I warned this man with perfumed skin
I challenged him to fight
I warned him that his perfumed skin
would not survive the night.
Stab. Feint. Stab again.
I said I would not quit
until I land upon this man
a palpable hit –

Referee Halte!

No result. They separate.

Cyrano Last stanza.

Valvert You're a dead man.

Cyrano Make my day.

Referee En garde. – Prêts? – Allez.

They fight.

Cyrano My sword is long, not so my song,
my song is quick as steel.
Parry – riposte – the fight is lost
my friend – and no appeal.
I warned this man his perfumed skin
would separate and split
I warned this perfumed man I'd planned
to land upon his body with this hand –
the only language he can understand –
A PALPABLE HIT.

On the word 'hit' Cyrano wounds the other man, who staggers back, bleeding.

Fetch him a doctor.

——   Amazing!

——   Amazing skill!

—— You think? But using poetry to actually kill someone –

Cyrano   He's not going to die – he just needs stitches.

—— His poems or his sword – I don't know which is more dangerous.

——   It doesn't seem humanly possible –

—— He's losing blood!
                Let's get this man please to the hospital!

Valvert's friends take him out. Cyrano seems preoccupied.

Leila Cyrano? You okay?

Le Bret   Come on: I say the winner takes us all out and pays for a posh dinner.

—— Cyrano?

Cyrano   What?

——   You were amazing.

Cyrano   Oh?

—— That palpable hit bit.

Le Bret   Shall we go?
    Cyrano?

Leila   He isn't listening.

——   After everything he's done he needs a drink.

Le Bret   Cyrano. Dinner.

Cyrano (*smiles*)   Got no money.

Pause.

Le Bret No money? But you just bought out the house –
                              that wad of cash –

Cyrano (*smiles*) – was my life-savings.
                    I've nothing left. Only my own panache.

Pause. Ragueneau goes up to him.

What's this, Leila?

Leila   You need to eat.
Small flask of brandy plus something sweet
for later. Get some sleep.

Cyrano Thank you.

———   Okay everybody – clear the stage –
we're going dark! –

*Other stage hands repeat the warning 'Going dark!
Going dark!' The lights dim. Everyone drifts out
chatting . . .*

———   . . . his use of language
is quite distinctive.

———   Yes but I'd be surprised
if that palpable hit thing was genuinely improvised . . .

. . . *leaving Cyrano alone with Le Bret.*

Le Bret Well – talk about rising to the bait –
red rag to the bull – you've just displayed
appallingly poor judgement. Why
did you have to fight like that? That man could die.

Cyrano I was provoked.

Le Bret   Provoked – maybe – but influential people
  may well judge otherwise.

Cyrano   I know: I'm evil.

Le Bret Plus you do realise Richelieu –

Cyrano   Was the Cardinal there?

Le Bret Yes he was – and you need to take care –
  those are the wrong kinds of enemies to make.

Cyrano The Cardinal – (*Smiles.*) yes that was a mistake.
  But when it comes to acting
  he's pretty exacting:
  you're not telling me
  he'd support Montfleury –

Le Bret Maybe not – but it's all the others too –
  de Guiche – the patrons. It's like all you can do
  is cause trouble.
  You can't exist in this self-contained bubble –
  embrace the system – start to engage –
  make alliances – don't just rage.
  You have no proper insight
  into your actions – pick fight after pointless fight –
  insult people – obstruct them – adopt this pose of . . .

 Cyrano My system's simple: I follow my nose.
  This nose – look – is the perfect moral compass:
  it points to the truth, and significant numbers
  of fools are spiked on its gleaming tip.
  My system is simple: don't think, just let rip.

 Le Bret But why Montfleury? – some wretched actor –
  what is the so-called moral factor there?

 Cyrano Disgust.
  Montfleury's the embodiment of flabbiness and lust.
  I've watched him – in his actorly disguise –
  undressing a particular young woman with his eyes –

a particular young woman – yes –
watched the slime of his gaze slide over her dress.

Le Bret Particular young woman? – who?
Somebody you happen to be attracted to?

Cyrano
And why should I not be 'attracted'? It's bad enough
to be ugly – but to be ugly and in love . . .
And at the same time love the one woman
whose beauty's so luminous it's beyond the human.

Pause.

Le Bret I see. Roxane.

Cyrano And I can't even talk to her like a normal man.

Le Bret Rubbish. If you're in love with her just tell her.

Cyrano Oh sure, sure, that's a hell of an
easy thing to say – but where do I start?
I have this thing – this nose, remember? –
                              between me and every woman's heart.
You know, sometimes I go out walking.
It's evening. There in a garden talking
are young men and women holding hands.
I think: that looks so easy. Each seems to understand
the other. They have an effortless connection.
They smile. Smell the roses. Fear of rejection
never enters their minds. Their god is
flesh. They're confident in their young
                              and attractive bodies.
I think: I'm like that too – young and desirable.
And then I see my shadow on the garden wall.

Le Bret Come on, Cyrano, spare me the self-pity.
Girls get that shit – men don't need to be pretty.
Plus – like it or not –
seeing men fight gets women hot –

you think when you were fighting your . . . your . . .
                                        your poetry duel
she wasn't up there watching you?
Get real. Roxane's
a grown-up – she wants a man.

Cyrano I'm not convinced.

Le Bret   I'd offer guarantees
you figure in any number of her sexual fantasies.
Sure, she's really really beautiful –
that doesn't mean put her on a pedestal.
Come on, man. Get in there. Attack.

Woman Excuse me. Is one of you gentlemen
                                        Cyrano de Bergerac?

Pause. A Woman has appeared.

Cyrano That's me.

Woman   Of course – yes – the nose – sorry.
Well the thing is is somebody has asked me
if you would be able to meet her privately
tomorrow morning – and she really underlines
privately. Oh and she suggests a time:
seven a.m. How would that suit?

Cyrano Somebody being?

Woman   Or she could do it
later – but seven ideally if you can.

Cyrano Somebody being?

Woman   Oh did I not say? – Roxane.

Pause.

Cyrano Roxane wants to meet me.

Woman   In private, please.

28

Cyrano In private.

Woman   Yes, that's the normal thing
                                        in situations such as these.

Cyrano Situations.

Woman   Yes, and she's asking do you know
  the cake-stroke-café-bookshop
                                        run by Leila Ragueneau?

Cyrano Of course.

Woman   That's where she'll be then. Come at seven.

  The Woman goes.

Le Bret Well? See the effect you have on women?

Cyrano She wants to meet me! Coffee! Books!

Le Bret
  Told you – they really don't care how a man looks.

Cyrano
  I'm   I'm   I'm   SO FUCKING HAPPY! This is it –
  this is my total dream come true – SHIT!

Le Bret So now maybe try to relax.

Cyrano   RELAX?
  I'm going to get out there with a with a
                                        with a fucking AXE!

Le Bret Cyrano – please – bit of calm.

Cyrano
  But this is a total mindfuck – breakfast with Roxane.

  *Lignière appears in full flow of language. He seems
  high.*

Lignière Yeah show me your face
  keep up the pace

29

of the Parisian master-race
I don't got no place here
hey clear me some empty space here

Cyrano Lignière?

Lignière They tell me the end
they tell me this is the end my friend
they tell me what they send
they gonna send one hundred men
they gonna cut my face
they gonna put this harassed Paris poet in his place –
claims that I've named him
claims I've defamed him
keep every writer on a leash
this is the order of de Guiche –

Cyrano Lignière?

Lignière De Guiche is the man who polices speech
who tells the hundred men to teach
the poet not to overreach –
cut me cut me – teach me a lesson –
cut my face – get my confession –

Cyrano Lignière?

Lignière Pull out the knife – turn up the heat –
they gonna beat this man on the Paris street
cut me cut me – come on now try it
show me a rule I will defy it
I wrote the words I won't deny it
cut my face – bring on the riot
BRING ON THE RIOT!

*Lignière suddenly goes blank and sways. The others
hold him up.*

Cyrano A hundred men? Where?

Lignière I'm telling you, man. They are OUT THERE.
Outside some bar
near the Pont des Arts.

Cyrano If there really are a hundred men,
stay here – and I will deal with them.

Le Bret Cyrano –

Cyrano   What?

Le Bret   He's off his face.

Cyrano
Sure – which is why I intend to go there in his place.
If de Guiche thinks he can silence writers
he needs to understand that some of us are fighters:
I'll give those hundred men a lesson
in free-speech and the writer's right to self-expression.
You can watch. You can shout all you like and scream.
But please: not a single one of you 's to intervene.

Le Bret Cyrano, don't. They'll kill you.

Cyrano   Kill me? Oh?
Scum sent by de Guiche? – you think so? No.
Down to the Seine! Down to the Pont des Arts!
You think I care how many men there are?
Ten or ten thousand, I shall defend
the life and writing of my poet friend.

Act Two

*Seven a.m. Madame Ragueneau is running an early
morning cookery and creative-writing course for a small
number of students of all ages.*

Leila Now – precious friends – before you all start
  writing I want you to consider this
                          traditional French lemon tart.

What connections can we see between our poetry
and the fine art of patisserie?

Is it that both feed the soul?

Or is it more technical?

Is it the form? Is it the position
of each in relation to a tradition?

When I created the lemon-curd, I mixed butter and eggs:
could this be compared to the lexical effects
of adjective mixed with noun?

Or take vanilla. Look – the pod is a rich black-brown.
But if I use ingredients from a distant nation
am I then guilty of – what shall we call it? –
                          cultural appropriation?

Do such borrowings in writing amount to theft?
Or would there – without borrowing – be nothing left?
Who can cook what? This lemon tart
reminds us of the rich community of art.

Questions?

32

A hand goes up.

Marie-Louise – yes.

Marie-Louise I'm really into the curd
I think curd's such a great word
the word curd really needs to get heard
and that bit earlier when you stirred the curd
that was cool. Brilliant!

Leila Thank you, Marie-Louise – thank you immensely –
just remember the things you write
       don't have to always rhyme quite so intensely.

Laughter. A hand goes up.

Yes – what can I do for you, Armande?

Armande I really like cakes – plus I'm really fond
of pastries. But I feel like today's society can make
poets really self-conscious about their body-shape.

Leila Fair point, Armande. It didn't used to be
like this – poets' bodies got far less scrutiny –
but this is the 1640s and I'm afraid
our appearance is now part of our stock-in-trade:
body-mass – weight-loss – fashionable clothes –
or simply – I don't know –
       simply just having a sticking-out nose.

Laughter. Hands go up.

Yes – Denise.

Denise   Do poems have to rhyme?

Laughter.

Leila I'm afraid so, Denise. Not that there wasn't a time
when they didn't: Virgil – the Ancient Greeks –
a poet speaks
to us in different ways.

But when it comes to people like us –

                    modern people nowadays –

we can't simply veto
rhyme and metre.

Marie-Louise Why not?

Leila   Well, Marie-Louise,
as I was saying to Denise,
rhymes just like classic recipes
such as these
have been found to please
the majority of French people so
that's what we do. Now pick up your pencils
                and off you go. [*i.e. start writing.*]

And remember, your poems will be all the better for
a well-developed food-based metaphor.

*The students begin to write in silence. After a while
Cyrano enters, and a quiet conversation with
Ragueneau begins.*

Cyrano. Welcome. What can I get you?

Cyrano Coffee, Leila. And a shot of brandy.

Leila   I bet you've
been up all night.

Cyrano   Maybe.

Leila   These are the stars
of my early morning writing-class.

*Pause. She serves a coffee and brandy for them both.
They clink glasses. The student writers continue to
write.*

Cyrano Santé.

Leila   Santé. What's happened to your hand?

Cyrano Nothing. Accident.

Leila   Okay.

  Pause.

Cyrano   Listen, Leila, I was actually planning
  to meet someone.

Leila   Now?

Cyrano   Yes – would you be able
  to give the two of us some sort of private table?

Leila Of course. Better than that –
  I can take these guys through
                              into the kitchen at the back.

Cyrano
  Thank you. First there's something I've got to write.

Leila Cake?

Cyrano   Love to – love to, Leila, but I've got no appetite.

  *Cyrano starts writing. Ragueneau attends to her
  students. All speak sotto voce.*

—— They say he was involved in a serious fight.

Leila Cyrano?

——   Yeah – happened last night
  near the Pont des Arts –

Cyrano (*writing*)
  '*Venus . . . moonlight . . . the evening star . . .*'

—— Some kind of gang – seven dead –

—— Seven?

——   That's what this friend of my husband said.

Leila Concentrate on your poems please.

Cyrano (*writing*) '. . . *on evenings, Roxane . . .*
on nights like these . . .'

This is just bullshit.

He screws up the paper and takes another piece.

Leila   Another brandy?

Cyrano   Yup.

———   Sure it was him?

——— (*taps nose*) Unless he's got an identical twin –

Leila
No more talking, please. You have five more minutes.

She serves the brandy.

Cyrano (*writing*) '. . . *Roxane . . . I don't know how*
to begin this . . .
your existence . . . has changed
the whole world for me . . .'

——— There's this girl he likes at the University –

Leila Hush now. No gossip.

———   What can I make rhyme with kiss?

Cyrano (*writing*) '*I'm terrified to speak, Roxane . . .*
that's why I'm writing this . . .'

Leila Miss – Bliss – use your intelligence –
or Less – maybe Bless – they work by assonance –

——— Like Undress –

Leila   Like Undress, Denise – thank you – yes.

Cyrano (*writing*)
'*I love you . . . but it's so hard to express . . .*
I'm . . . suspicious of clichés . . . I'm . . . I'm . . .'

Leila Okay, everyone – nearly time –

36

Cyrano (*writing*) '*I love you, Roxane . . .*
if I could speak, I'd've said . . .
I want you . . . and I want . . . to wake up
beside you every morning in your bed . . .'

Roxane appears.

*The students see her first and freeze in wonder at her
beauty. Then Cyrano notices and quickly hides away
the letter in his pocket.*

Leila Roxane – lovely to see you – are you well?

Roxane Mmm – Leila – what is that wonderful smell?

Leila Lemon tart.

Pause.

Okay, everybody, we're going to start
reading each other's poems –
but we will do it through here.
Yes yes – she's beautiful – try not to stare.
I'm so sorry.

Roxane   No worries.

Leila   Come on you people – out.
If you need cakes – books – coffee –
anything – more brandy – give me a shout.

Ragueneau and the writers leave the room.
Pause.

Roxane They looked like scared rabbits!

Cyrano They've lots to learn. These would-be writers
have some pretty unappealing habits.

Pause.

Coffee?

Roxane No. Thank you.

Cyrano   Or a drink?

Roxane Seven a.m. – a little early for me, I think.

Pause.

Cool place – Leila's so into poetry.

Cyrano Look – Roxane – this . . . (how can I put this?) –
this really is a very special moment for me.

Pause.

Roxane For me too.

Cyrano   May I assume you're here today
because there's something . . . special or . . .
particularly important that you'd like to say?

Roxane There is. And first off – thank you. Because
that little shit
you beat in yesterday's duel was the man de Guiche
saw fit

to make me marry. That's right: I marry Valvert,
Valvert leases me back to de Guiche. Job-share
for them – sex-slavery for me – but now they won't dare.
So thank you: Valvert lost his appetite
for that little plan when he lost the fight.

Cyrano nods to acknowledge her thanks.

Second – I've something even more . . . intimate
to confess –
and I don't know how to begin this – unless
you remember us both being little? We were so close.
Like brother and sister. You'd be wounded –
I'd be nurse:
typical girl-boy stuff. I liked dreaming –

Cyrano
While I rushed round waving a stick and screaming? –

Roxane That kind of thing – or trying to torture my cat.

38

Cyrano Shit, was I really as bad as that?

Roxane You were a boy, that's all. And I could be spiteful back – it doesn't mean I didn't like you.

Pause.

Has something happened to your hand?

Cyrano No. Just a scratch. But I don't understand / what –

Roxane Just a scratch? Show me. It's deep!

Perhaps she keeps hold of his hand through what follows.

Cyrano Please.

Roxane   Shall I clean it?

Cyrano   No – no – listen to me – please –

Roxane Did you really take on a hundred men? –

Cyrano Please – what was it you meant when you said more intimate? – when you said confess?

Pause.

Roxane You want me to say?

Cyrano   Well of course I do. Yes.

Pause.

Roxane
Well – it's like this – we're not little kids any more – and there is someone – a man – I have
                        very strong feelings for.

Cyrano Strong feelings.

Roxane   Very. But this . . . person doesn't know.

Pause.

Cyrano You love this person.

Roxane   Yes. Yes. I love him so

incredibly and I know that he loves me too
                              but that he's afraid to speak.

Pause.

Cyrano You love him.

Roxane   Yes. And week after week
   I've heard how this . . . person looks at me then turns
      away.
   I just wish he would come out with it and say
   what he really feels.

Cyrano   What he really feels – of course he should – yes.

Roxane
   And he's a soldier – exactly like you are – in the cadets –

Cyrano – exactly like me –

Roxane   — yes, exactly! – like some dream! –
   Plus he's the most good-looking boy I have ever ever
      seen.

*Pause. If she is still holding it, Cyrano gently takes
away his hand.*

Something wrong?

Cyrano shakes his head.

                  And it was love at first sight
   because I'd never even *seen* him before last night.

Cyrano Last night?

Roxane   At the play.

Cyrano   So – sorry – how d'you know? –

Roxane – he loves me? Because all of my friends 've
                                    told me so –
   seems it's embarrassingly self-evident.

Cyrano
And this . . . whatever . . . person – is in my regiment?

Roxane Yes!

Cyrano   What's his name?

Roxane   Christian.

Cyrano Can't be. Never heard of the man.

Roxane
Ah, but he only enrolled, don't you see, this morning.

Pause.

Cyrano Roxane –

Roxane   Yes?

Cyrano   Roxane, I know that falling
in love can be sudden.
                  But you live for poetry and books –
what if his intelligence fails to match his looks?

Roxane It won't. That isn't possible. It's *meant to be*.
He's mine, Cyrano – physically and intellectually.

Pause.

Something wrong?

Cyrano   No . . . sorry . . . I'm not quite clear
exactly why, Roxane, why you have asked me here.

Roxane Well . . . I know you Gascons can't abide a
guy like Christian – bit of an outsider –

Cyrano Too right.

Roxane   – and less of a big mouth
than all you nut-jobs from the South –

Cyrano Thank you.

Roxane   – present company of course excepted –

and the thing is is I've heard he can expect
to be bullied – and worse – forced to suffer in silence
all kinds of weird macho power-games and violence.

Cyrano It's the army.

Roxane   Yes. But *you* might decide
to reserve that violence – if I ask you really nicely –
                              for the other side.

Pause.

Cyrano You'd like me to protect him.

Roxane   Would you? Please?

Cyrano Of course.

Roxane   Thank you!

Cyrano   Of course I will – he's . . .

Roxane He's such a special person. Be his friend.

Cyrano I promise.

Roxane   No bullying then? – or duelling?

Cyrano   No violence. End
of story.

Roxane   Thank you so much. I really ought to go.

Cyrano That's fine.

Roxane   Oh and I so much wanted to know
about your fight. A hundred men – amazing!

Cyrano Another time.

Roxane   And you didn't mind me raising
this subject?

Cyrano   Not at all.

Roxane   You're so sweet – I sensed it would be alright.

Pause.

Oh and one last thing: get Christian to write.

Cyrano No problem.

Roxane
Isn't this great? Like we've gone back to being little –
you with your sticks of wood –

                            me with my dolls' hospital.

Cyrano Yes, marvellous.

Roxane   You will tell him: write to me.

Cyrano Of course I will. Immediately.

Roxane I really appreciate this, Cyrano.

Cyrano It's nothing.

*Pause. She sees something's wrong, but doesn't
understand what it is.*

Roxane   Look – forgive me but I've got to go.

She leaves.
  For some moments Cyrano is alone.
  Then a commotion, and a group of soldiers appear.

—— Where is he?

——   Cyrano!

——   Cyrano! Three cheers
for our mighty swordsman!

——   Crack open the beers!

—— Hip hip.

——   HOORAY!

——   Hip hip.

——   HOORAY!

——   Hip hip.

43

—— HOORAY!

——   Clothes off everybody! Strip!

—— (*chant*) Strip! Strip! Strip! Strip!

Some of the men get naked.
  Madame Ragueneau and her writers come back in
and watch with amusement.

—— Who's the man we always back?

—— CYRANO DE BERGERAC!

—— Who can take the fucking flak?

—— CYRANO DE BERGERAC!

—— Who is it the twats attack?

—— CYRANO DE BERGERAC!

—— Here we go.

—— CYRANO!

—— Our hero.

—— CYRANO!

—— Who would go to hell and back?

—— CYRANO! CYRANO! CYRANO DE BERGERAC!

Mayhem. The men try and fête an unwilling Cyrano.

De Guiche appears.

Eventual silence.

De Guiche Well I had no idea that our humble soldiery
took so much interest in books and poetry.

Pause.

Leila
  They're always welcome. Books – just like good food –
                          can be enjoyed by everyone, you know.

De Guiche Yes thank you for your insipid humanism,
   Madame Ragueneau.
  But I can assure you: without me here to govern
  them they'd take these books of yours
                 and burn them in that oven.
  Cyrano – I offer you my admiration –
  a hundred men – clearly an occasion
  to celebrate –

—— Hip hip –

De Guiche   NOT that I would choose to see
  normally
  quite this degree
  of vigorous male nudity
  before breakfast.
                But – joking apart –
  Cyrano, I admire you. You have heart.
  You're fearless. I've also heard you have ambitions
  as a writer and the fact is I'm in a position
  to help.

Cyrano   I don't need any help writing – thank you.

De Guiche Very good – but the thing is
    even some of the writers in this class outrank you –
  you lack sponsorship and literary connections
  and no one these days can write
                without sponsors and protection.
  I repeat: I can help. But most significantly of all,
  so can my uncle, the Cardinal.

Cyrano Richelieu?

De Guiche   No less. Your bravura's brought you
  to his attention and he is prepared now to support you:
  poems – plays – please – show him your writing.

Pause.

Leila Cyrano. Do it.

Cyrano (*tempted*) You mean he's actually inviting / me to –

De Guiche Yes. Yes. Show him your work. He arranges
  publication –

Cyrano (*more tempted*) Publication –

De Guiche   – yes and personally helps a writer
                        make the necessary changes.

  Pause.

Cyrano Changes.

De Guiche   Well yes – especially with plays –
  he'll help you identify and cut redundant
                                or offensive phrases.

Cyrano Offensive.

De Guiche   Political incorrectness – vulgarity –
  that kind of thing. A writer's vanity
  can make him forget that certain basic rules of decency
    apply.

Cyrano I will change *nothing* – I would rather *die*.

De Guiche Oh really?

Cyrano   You think that's funny?

De Guiche
  Not at all. But the Cardinal actually pays money –
  money, Cyrano. Just think carefully before you decide.
  You're proud –

Cyrano   Too right.

De Guiche   – but no one can live off pride.

A soldier comes in with some blood-stained rubbish-bags.

What the hell is that?

————   Personal effects.
Ninety-three ran off – but there were seven deaths.
Sorry about the blood. And not just your average yob:
this was high-class rent-a-mob.

———— But who was the stupid cunt sent them?

————   I'd so love to see
the look on his face now.

De Guiche   The stupid cunt was me.

Slight pause.

Yes they were to remind that self-styled 'poet' Lignière
to take a little more care
before making his defamatory attacks.

Leila Lignière?

Cyrano   Lignière – Monsieur de Guiche –
                                simply reports the facts.

De Guiche I've had enough of this. We're leaving.
If you think you're morally superior you are deceiving
yourself. Who tilts at windmills, Cyrano?
                                Idealists – fools –
people who don't understand society has rules.
Pick fights with windmills and those rotating bars
will drag you through cow-shit –

Cyrano   – or propel me towards the stars.

De Guiche leaves with his entourage.

Leila Well Cyrano, never let it be said
you miss an opportunity to shoot yourself in the head.

Cyrano My brains are intact, thank you.

Le Bret   But your mind –
what were you *thinking of*?

Cyrano   I'm resigned
to self-destruction. How could I *begin*
to accept 'protection' from a man like him?

Leila But the Cardinal – I'm sorry but that's suicide.

Cyrano
So you too – is this right? – are accusing me of pride?
What is it you want from me? –
some kind of deference? How can I be
myself without my 'political incorrectness' and
    'vulgarity'?
Yes yes I'm well aware I don't stand much of a chance
here in the literary world of seventeenth-century France –
money – cronyism – fear of giving offence –
poets on juries awarding cash-prizes to their friends.
As for our seventeenth-century theatre – well – don't
    you agree
it's become just fly-paper for mediocrity? –
sure, you can set the bar quite high –
but still the writers stick on it and die –
and even dead they offer thanks
to all their sponsors – to the banks
and banks' best mates
who've managed to manipulate the interest rates –
then add for peanuts to their shopping cart
the priceless prestige that they derive from art.
I mean why would I even have a conversation
with this Cardinal? Publication? –

Leila Cyrano – stop this.

Cyrano   No – let me speak –
he'd simply crush in my voice
                              everything that is unique –

48

just like he'd take all of you aspiring writers
cut up your work and leave just the dead detritus.

Leila Cyrano.

Cyrano   Do not Cyrano me.
To be myself, I need to be free –

Le Bret Free is one thing – but you actually set out
to make enemies. What's that about?

Cyrano I need them, Le Bret – I need their hate –
let them stare – let them spit with rage – I can't wait
for the next fight –
no way will I kowtow and be polite –
try and make me
conform try and break me
I warn you no one will take me
prisoner of their patronage
VIP sponsorship whatever the fashion is
I will remain outside of it
will not stain any part of my mind with it
I will sing to my own tune
cling to the dark side of my own moon
sooner than bask in the false bright
earth-light
offer no remedies to my many enemies
I need them, Le Bret, I need that hate
need them to isolate
me SO THAT I CAN CREATE.

Everyone looks in shocked silence at Cyrano.
  Christian enters unnoticed.
  Madame Ragueneau takes Cyrano gently aside.

Leila Cyrano – listen – I know you feel strongly but can
I just ask: did something happen with Roxane?

Cyrano turns away.

—— Cyrano! Quite some speech!

—— But don't beat yourself up so much
                              about de Guiche –

—— Such a loser.

——   Hey tell us about that fight!

Cyrano
    Just give me a couple of minutes, gentlemen – alright?
    He talks privately to Madame Ragueneau.

—— (*to Christian*) Thing is, new boy,
                              is he gets like this –

—— Especially if he thinks (*Taps nose.*) you're taking
    the piss.

Christian You mean the . . . ?

——   Exactly. And whatever you do:
    don't say it.

Christian   You mean –?

——   Shh! The word is taboo.
    Slight pause.

Christian I can't say / nose?

——   Shh! – he'll kill you soon
    as you mention . . .

——   . . . the elephant in the room.
    Slight pause.

Christian Elephant?

——   Shh! – total news blackout applies
    both to the organ and to any mention
                              of its prodigious size.

—— If he gets the slightest whiff of piss-take
    you're a dead man.

——   Big mistake.

—— Not just injured,
mate – but fucking skewered.
Got the picture?

Pause.

Christian   Could he not get a nose-job?

—— SHH!

—— Not when you've got the full-length garden hose job
like that.

Cyrano   Okay. I'm ready. Gather round.

—— (*sotto*) Don't get too clever, new boy.
                              Last recruit was found
with most of a bottle shoved up his arse.

Christian (*sotto*) Like you then, was he: bottom of the
class?

—— (*sotto*) I've got your number.

Christian (*sotto*)   I don't scare
so easily.

—(*sotto*) Sure. But Cyrano? – you wouldn't dare.

Christian (*sotto*) Try me.

Cyrano   Okay, everybody. Ready to roll.

—— (*all chant*) CYRANO! CYRANO! CYRANO!
CYRANO!

Cyrano gestures good-naturedly for silence.
  Then sets out to deliver a gripping narrative.

Cyrano Night-time – picture me – alone in the moonlight –
down by the river – fired-up – ready to fight.
The moon gleams like a yellow clock-face
                              and the wide night
sky glitters with stars.

51

Pause.

Denise (*sotto*)   Wide night sky – that's really great.

Leila (*sotto*)
  Simple and clear, Denise – technique to imitate.

Cyrano Then clouds piled in a vast stack
  roll out over Paris and the light fades pink –
                fades orange – then it dims to black.
  One moment the moon's yellow clock-face glows:
  the next I can't see –

Christian   – past the end of my nose.

*Silence. Everyone looks at Cyrano, expecting a
reaction, but there is only further silence.*

Cyrano Who is this person?

Le Bret   New boy. Just came.

—— Arrived this morning.

Cyrano   This morning.

Le Bret   Yes his name –

Christian I'm Christian.

Cyrano   Christian?

*Cyrano looks like he might attack Christian – but
makes a huge effort to control himself.*

          Christian – right – good – yes –
                so – as I was saying . . .
  One moment the moon's yellow clock-face glows
  and the next – *Jesus!* – the next I can't see –
                since the darkness that ebbed – now flows.

*Pause. General amazement that Cyrano hasn't risen to
the bait.*

So there I am – aware that defending
                            my poet-friend's case is
going to make me enemies in very high places:
I know I will get up –

Christian   – somebody's nose –

Cyrano (*with immense self-control*) – the next morning –
                    I know I will get up the *next morning*
and find I'm persona non grata. Then without warning
be given –

Christian   – a bloody nose –

Cyrano   – a *summons* to appear
in front of de Guiche.
                    Yes this fight's going to cost me dear,
I'm thinking, but there's no – no there's no going back.

Pause.

Then suddenly – from the Pont des Arts – comes –

Christian   – a nasal attack –

Cyrano   VICIOUS – a VICIOUS attack.
I draw. I turn. And my God that is when
I find I'm confronting over a hundred men
all drunk. I charge like an animal –

Christian   – his nostrils flare –

Cyrano   – head-down – parry – thrust – I tear
through flesh – slash one – slash two –
                            fatally wound another –
slip on blood – stumble – fall – stagger – recover –
hack fifty down with a sequence of fifty blows –
then skewer ten more –

Christian   – on the end of my long
                            and exceptionally pointy nose.

Brief pause, then Cyrano explodes.

Cyrano JESUS CHRIST! OUT! ALL OF YOU OUT!
WELL? WHAT'RE YOU WAITING FOR?

—— (*to Christian*) You were warned, mate.
                                    There'll be blood on the floor.

Everyone goes, leaving Cyrano alone with Christian.
Pause.

Cyrano Embrace me. Bravo. Amazing guts.

Christian But I don't / understand –

Cyrano   Do it. Embrace me. No ifs, no buts.
I like you. You're brave – you've got proper spirit.

Christian Embrace you? Well . . .

Cyrano   Shut up, man – just do it.

They embrace.

Perhaps you don't realise who I am.

Christian What? You're Cyrano.

Cyrano   I'm her cousin, Christian.

Christian Cousin?

Cyrano   Don't you know who I mean?

Christian Roxane?

Cyrano   Exactly. So I know that you've been
– how shall I put this? – noticed. Yes in fact
she's quite smitten.

Christian   She loves me?

Cyrano   You could say that.

Pause.

Christian Incredible! Thank you! I'm totally amazed!

Cyrano You're a good-looking boy. Roxane has taste.

Christian But you – oh God – I so so admire you.

Cyrano Yes, and my nose, I've noticed
seems particularly to inspire you.

Christian I take all the noses back.

Cyrano   Yes yes – I'm sure – whatever.

Slight pause.

The thing is, Christian, she's expecting a letter.

Christian Roxane? A letter?

Cyrano   Yes – letter – tonight.

Christian I don't do letters – I can hardly write!

Cyrano Oh? When it came to attacking me
you seemed to express yourself pretty fluently.

Christian That's with men – they're easy to attack –
with men it's straightforward – but what I totally lack
is confidence with women. I balk
at the whole idea of having to write letters
                     or talk the talk.

Cyrano Talk the talk? Do you not mean set on fire
the obscure object of your heart's
                     still more obscure desire?

Christian Exactly. It's the stuff like that that I cannot do –
I don't have that gift – I'm not like you.

Cyrano
Well I have the gift – but unfortunately not the looks –

Christian And Roxane's so . . . highbrow –
                     she's totally obsessed by books.

55

Pause. Cyrano reflects.

Cyrano Look. I have a proposal. What I mean
is that together we could make a winning team:
you share with me your extremely pretty face –
I share with you my oh-so sophisticated turns of phrase.

Christian *What?*

Cyrano   Basically, I teach you what to say –
I give you lessons – one or two each day –

Christian *Lessons?*

Cyrano   Hear me out – yes I will produce the
words with which *you* can then seduce her.

Christian You're mad.

Cyrano   Oh do you think so? – mad? –
because I would say this is the best idea I've ever had –

Christian No.

Cyrano   – to see her laugh – dance – kiss –
                                    whatever – cry –
all according to a script that I myself supply.

Pause. Christian is disturbed by Cyrano's enthusiasm.

Come on, Christian – a partnership – say yes.

Christian
Partnership? – what exactly is it you get out of this?

Cyrano Get out of it? Me? (*Disingenuous.*) Nothing at all.
An opportunity to hone my skills. But it's your call.

Pause.

Christian
It's weird – but well – I need your help – so . . . Okay.

Cyrano Good.

56

Christian   Now about the letter

Cyrano   – the one she needs today.

Christian Exactly – can you give me some kind of steer?

Cyrano No need. I already have your letter here.

Cyrano produces the letter he wrote earlier.

Christian What's that?

Cyrano   Your letter – see? Don't stress.
Just put her name here, plus the address.

Christian How did you . . . ?

Cyrano   Oh, all of us on the poetry scene
make random samples – know what I mean? –
invent stuff – for competition-winning –
love-songs and so on to imaginary men and women.
Did you not know? Especially men like me
who are – well – often less fortunate – romantically.

Christian But that's not real – I can't – it's fake, it's –

Cyrano Not fake at all. Trust me. Take it.

Cautiously, Christian takes the letter.

Christian But if she found out – it could be full of lies –

Cyrano There are no lies in the letter. Everything applies
strictly to Roxane. I would be happy to defend
every line. Believe me. As a friend.

Christian You've saved my life.

Christian impulsively hugs Cyrano.
Madame Ragueneau, soldiers, and student writers
reappear and watch.

——   I do not believe this.

—— What the fuck? He's taking the piss.
Cyrano? Cyrano?

Cyrano   I'd like you to meet my best friend
Christian. He's a star. Shake his hand.

—— What?

——   Shake his hand? But all those . . .
insults – Cyrano? – (*Lowers voice.*) the nose.

Cyrano Shake his hand please.

They do so.

——   Congratulations, mate.

—— So the nose is fair game now – is that right? – great!

Cyrano Fair game?

—— (*with increasing bravado*) Yeah, the way it juts out
                              like I don't know what –

—— Like a stick –

——   Like a stick – like a pick –

——   Like a stick of rock –

—— Like a rod – like a pipe –

——   Like a greasy pole
or mast of a ship –

——   Like a whole
load of sticky-out things –

——   Like chips –

*Cyrano starts to walk quietly away. Christian watches
him.*

—— Yeah, really big chips or like fruit full of pips –

—— pippy –

58

—— and full of that wet kind of string –
kind of really big orangey pulpy thing –

—— like mangoes –

—— or kumquats –

—— or kumquats?
A kumquat is tiny –

—— Okay well that's –

—— Cyrano! Hey! Don't go. What's wrong?

—— Well maybe not kumquat.

Christian   He's crazy.

Leila   He's gone.

Act Three

Roxane's house. Two exits: one to outside, one to an inner room.

Roxane, De Guiche.

Roxane What is it you want?

De Guiche I've come to say goodbye.

Roxane Well – okay – goodbye then.

De Guiche Are you not going to ask me why?

Roxane Yes of course. You're leaving . . . Whatever for?

De Guiche
We're being mobilised, Roxane. Mobilised. It's war.

Roxane War! How exciting!

De Guiche I wanted you to know.

Pause.

You don't seem to care much.

Roxane Of course I care. Bravo!
Bravo, de Guiche – my thoughts are with you.

De Guiche I've brought you this.

Roxane Oh?

De Guiche Yes – a picture of myself – to give you.

Roxane Thank you. Well. Amazing. War. Whatever next.

De Guiche They're also putting me, Roxane,
in charge of the cadets.

Roxane (*alert*) Cadets?

De Guiche
 Yes – and I intend to keep them on their toes
 particularly since I'll be commanding your cousin
      with the – whatever – with the nose.

Roxane Cyrano?

De Guiche   Yes – and I shan't spare him.

Slight pause.

 You're not close, I hope?

Roxane   No no – not at all – can't bear him.

De Guiche Good. Plus he's always going round
 with that pretty new boy on the parade ground –
 what's his name – Christi something –

Roxane   Christi something – is he?

De Guiche Well this is war – and 'scuse my French
      but I will keep the motherfucker busy.

Slight pause.

Roxane So when you say not spare him . . .

De Guiche   Yes?

Roxane   . . . you mean
 put him deliberately in danger.

De Guiche   I do.

Roxane   But isn't that his dream?
 Cyrano lives for danger – he loves to fight –
 loves having some overwhelming enemy in sight:
 the mental rush – adrenalin – the heaps of dead . . .
 Why not just order him to stay back here instead?

De Guiche What?

Roxane
Keep his whole team back in Paris. Cut off his balls:
a week of that and he'll be climbing up the walls.

Pause.

De Guiche Brilliant.

Roxane   Thank you.

De Guiche   That's brilliant – he'll go mad.
That is the most twisted idea a woman ever had.

Roxane Thank you.

De Guiche   Keep them in Paris. Amazing plan.
Only a girl like you could totally emasculate a man.

Roxane Well, thank you.

Modestly acknowledging her genius for emasculation,
she smiles.
   Pause.

De Guiche   Roxane –

Roxane   Yes?

De Guiche   Might I take this to be a sign
of love?

Roxane Well . . . yes . . . in a way.

De Guiche   There's not much time
then. Listen. I'm supposed to be out on the road
tonight – sign papers – go to meetings – load
up weapons – brief my men –
but why would I want to do all that, Roxane, when
what we could actually do instead
is spend the next few hours together in bed.

Roxane In bed. Um . . .

De Guiche
  Yes don't worry – I know a priest and he keeps rooms
  not far from here – for the monks et cetera, one
      assumes –
  but since I'm like this with the Cardinal
  this priest would definitely be able to make one
      available
  to us – to you, Roxane – to you and me.
  What d'you say? I love you – I love you so passionately.

Roxane But isn't that – what's the word? – desertion?
                                                  What about the war?

De Guiche I'll take the risk. Just for one night.

Roxane   But the law –
  the military law, Antoine. Antoine, forgive me
  but I need the man I love to be a man –
                                        fight and have dignity.

  Pause.

De Guiche (*moved*) You used my name.

Roxane   Yes – yes I did, Antoine –
  and I would not say Antoine to just anyone.

  He kisses her hand.

De Guiche
  You're so damn right. My duty is to my regiment.

Roxane Exactly. That is exactly what I meant.
  Good luck, Antoine. And thank you for the picture.

  De Guiche leaves.
    Cyrano appears.

  Cyrano?

Cyrano   What did *he* want?

Roxane   (*suddenly remembering*)
                                    Oh God. I have a lecture.

Cyrano Lecture?

Roxane   Quite interesting. Or meant to be.
  'Women and the male gaze in early modern poetry'
  I think it's about to begin.
  Oh – and if Christian happens to pop in –

Cyrano Pop in?

Roxane   Yes – would you ask him to wait, please?

Cyrano Of course.

Roxane   I'm afraid I've been teasing
  him lots about his writing.

Cyrano Oh? – I thought everything about him
                              was totally bold and exciting.

Roxane (*smiles*) That's mean. No, it's just he goes
                      through these weird blank phases –
  then suddenly comes up with amazing amazing phrases.
  He's actually a genius.

Cyrano   Oh?

Roxane   And Cyrano – I love him – it such a cliché
  but it's true. Oh God now I'm so embarrassed I don't
    know what to say.

  Pause.

Cyrano His writing's really as good as that?

Roxane   Look I know
  he can come across as a bit slow
  but he's deep, Cyrano. There's this part
  of him that completely gets the human heart.
  You wouldn't believe the things he writes.

Cyrano Such as?

Roxane   I can't tell you that – but absolute insights

into love and what women want –
sorry, that's embarrassing – I can't
really explain – and not just intellectually –
other things too – everything – sexually.
And it's weird because he can also act completely stupid
then everyone's confused – myself included.

Cyrano Perhaps when he sees you he's simply overawed.

Roxane (*takes this as a joke*) Oh don't you start!
                                        I am so so bored
with not being taken seriously by men.
Not you – I'm sorry – you are my dearest
                              and most perfect friend.

Pause.

There is one thing though.

Cyrano   What's that?

Roxane   Well just
that Christian is sometimes . . . unspontaneous.
Like everything he says to me has kind of been prepared?
It's beautiful, but stiff. I'm not exactly scared –
but something's going on with him I can't quite analyse.
So tonight what I plan to do is make him improvise.

Cyrano Improvise?

Roxane
        You know – invent stuff – poetry – plunge right in.
I'm going to push hard – really provoke him.
What d'you think?

Cyrano   Go for it.

Roxane   Yes?
Cyrano, you're lovely. Let me give you a kiss.

She sees that Cyrano almost imperceptibly steps back.

What is it?

Cyrano   You had some kind of class?

Roxane Oh my God yes! – the lecture! – there's
                                                                so many exams we've got to pass!

Roxane hurries out.
    Long pause.
    Then Cyrano calls softly for Christian.

Cyrano Christian. Christian.

Christian appears from another room.

    Well, the bad news is you're not very spontaneous –
but the good news is you're friends with a sensitive
    genius.
And who is that genius? Me.

Christian   Why am I not amused.

Cyrano Come *on*. Lighten *up*. She's just a tiny bit confused
    — that's all — and needs you to 'improvise'.
    Okay. It's a challenge. But if you take my advice –

Christian   I'm not listening.

Cyrano   – take my advice – I'll get you to learn
    something that *sounds* spontaneous. Make you burn
    and burn with truly spontaneous feeling. So –
    let's begin now and memorise / one or two –

Christian   Memorise. No!

Cyrano What?

Christian I said no. I won't do it.

Cyrano   You're insane –
    at least memorise one or two / phrases first.

Christian   No – this game
    of ours is over. I won't play this part

any more. It was fine – yes – okay – at the start –
but if she is really in love with me
why can't I just talk to her simply and naturally?

Cyrano Uh-huh.

Christian   Because I am not completely stupid.
Sure, I can't embroider speech the way you did –
launch verbal arrows like some kind of Cupid –
and no doubt in her eyes a
man like myself is not the most perfect 'improviser' –
but you've taught me, Cyrano, a great deal:
how to write, speak, touch. I'm a man: I can feel.
I can do this alone – believe me – I know.

Sees Roxane coming back.

Shit, she's coming! She's coming – don't go!

*Cyrano goes into the other room. A moment later
Roxane appears.*

Roxane   Hey – Christian.

They look at each other. Pause.

I had a lecture but I got there too late.
The hall was empty.

Awkwardly, Christian tries to kiss her.

                              (*Gently.*) No no no no – wait.
Isn't there something you want to say to me?
I mean about love . . .

Christian   Sure.

Roxane   . . . some way to be
poetic and . . . original . . . but also from the heart?
Listen. I'm going to snap my fingers, then you start.

She snaps her fingers.

Christian I love you.

Roxane   Uh-huh – you love me – and?

Christian I will always love you.

Roxane   Always love me – okay – so d'you think
                              you could maybe expand?

Christian Expand?

Roxane   Please.

Christian   Well . . . I would be so happy if you –
Roxane – would say please that you loved me too.

Roxane 'Would say please that I loved you too.'

Christian   Yes.

Roxane   That's really it?
I mean in terms of poetry that is just abject shit.

Christian I'm sorry.

Roxane   Don't apologise – apologise is worse –
come on now – improvise – improvise –
                              dazzle me with verse.

Christian I want to kiss you.

Roxane   Okay – to kiss me – and?

Christian
I love you. Please. Is that so difficult to understand?

Roxane
It's too *easy* – that's the problem – I'm just so *bored*
with 'being loved' –

Christian Okay, not loved – you are – / you are . . . .

Roxane I'm what? what? what? – come on – 'adored'?

Christian Yes!

Roxane
Adored – that's just so crap. *One* it is not sublime –
and *two* I'm even having to supply you with the
    fucking rhyme!

Christian Roxane!

Roxane (*moving away*)
Yes yes – you love me – sure – whatever.
I'll tell you something: you're ugly like this. Never
speak to me again – not until you have
    something truly spontaneous and beautiful to say.

Christian Roxane! Roxane!

*Roxane moves away, sits, turns her back, and starts to
read a book.*
    Cyrano appears in the doorway.

Cyrano (*sotto*)   So how's the love-play?
Pleased I'm keeping out of your way?
Managed to dazzle her mind?

Christian   Fuck off.

Cyrano   I'm sorry?

Christian   Please – please help me find
something intelligent to say –

Cyrano Bit late now. Maybe
if you'd taken my advice . . . What?

Christian   Look.
She hates me. She'd rather read some stupid book!

Cyrano Keep your voice down. Come on: we can fix this –
you don't deserve it, but we can. The risk is
she won't engage. So restart the conversation and I'll
    stay near
and help.

Christian   I can't.

Cyrano   I'm right here.
  Do it. Come on.

Christian   Roxane? Roxane?

Roxane (*coldly, without turning*)   What is it?
  Thought we'd ended your pathetic unpoetic visit.

Christian Please can we talk.

Cyrano
      Gently, gently – make your voice more / intimate.

Roxane Talk? – how? – when you're totally inarticulate.

Christian Please.

Roxane   Plus have no idea about love.

Christian (*prompted throughout now by Cyrano*)
                              No idea?
  My whole mind is love – and my love,
                              like my mind, is clear.

Roxane Okay. But this 'clear mind' of yours –
  doesn't that just mean vacant?

Christian   My mind draws
  all its strength from you. You're its support.
  You are the object . . . of my . . . of my every thought.

Roxane Not bad – but women as objects – bit of a male-
      gaze cliché –

Christian Accepted. But in my defence . . . in my defence
                              let me say
  that love would be . . . would be very dreary
  if it – (*To Cyrano.*) what? – if it fell – if it fell victim
                              to the gaze of Theory.

Roxane
      Dreary Theory! Not bad! But what's this hesitation?
      Sounds like you're on drugs.

Cyrano (*now imitates Cyrano's voice*)
                              I don't take medication –
    just my words move far more slowly after dark.

Roxane Slowly? How weird is that? Mine hit their mark
    instantly.

Cyrano   Because their target's broad:
    wide – and as open – as my heart.

    Roxane makes to turn.

Christian No!

Cyrano   No! – don't turn round!

Roxane   Why not?

Cyrano   Just please don't look – I . . .

Roxane What d'you mean don't look? Why?

Cyrano Indulge me. Let's be like the blind
    and see each other in the dark spaces
                          of each other's mind.

    Pause.

Roxane So?

Cyrano   I see a woman in a summer dress.
    And you?

Roxane   A man – I see a man – you, Christian – unless –

Cyrano Unless what?

Roxane   I don't know – you're being strange –

Cyrano Strange?

Roxane   Yes, like a different person –

Cyrano   What? – have I changed?

Roxane Changed? – no – just your tone . . .

Cyrano
    Because this is the first time I have ever been alone
    with you –

Roxane . . . your tone of voice. What? That's not true –
    we've been alone before.

Cyrano   No no no no. This is new.
    This is exceptional. Sorry – I'm just so confused –
    I'm always expecting to be laughed at or abused.

Roxane Laughed at? Why?

Cyrano   Oh – oh – no reason –
    just that I try so hard to please then
    hate myself – it's too easy, Roxane, to skim:
    don't you think love is an altogether deeper thing?

Roxane Trying to please me is okay.

Cyrano   You're right –
    but could we not aim for that deeper thing tonight?

    *Pause. Perhaps sotto voce: Christian, 'What's going
    on?' Cyrano, 'Shut up – I know what I'm doing.'*

Roxane Trying to please is good. Don't be afraid
    of that. But words are the thing. I've made
    a rule: however attractive a man is,
    it's his words that count *and* they must be spontaneous.

Cyrano However attractive.

Roxane   Yes –
    if a man can't improvise, I'll be merciless.

Cyrano Could you love an ugly person then?

Roxane   Well of course –
    unless he's some kind of weasel or looks like
                  whatever – like a horse.
    Can I turn around now?

Cyrano No! So you're quite serious:
you wouldn't judge a man by his appearance?

Roxane I didn't say *that*. Plus I know men:
I know they score women out of ten –
and it's not for their intelligence.

Christian (*sotto*)
Get on with it. This has stopped making sense.

Cyrano I love you, Roxane.

Roxane I know. You said before.
But I'm a woman. I'm a woman – I want more.

Cyrano I can do that. But believe me, this is not an act,
and I am about to say things I cannot retract.

Roxane Oh? What things?

Pause.

Cyrano Well in no particular order . . .
I love you, I need you, I want you, I go to sleep
thinking about you and wake up with your voice
winding through my head, I look at you and I can't
focus, the whole world shimmers, I'm ashamed,
I'm angry, I'm in love, I'm mad, I'm happy, I'm dead,
I'm alive, I'm stupid, I'm tongue-tied, I'm writing
you letters, I'm tearing them up, I'm writing you
letters again, I'm idealising you, I'm humiliating
you, I'm undressing you, I'm looking into your eyes,
I'm kissing your eyes, I'm pressing you against a
wall, you're pushing back, you're pushing back, your
body wants mine, you kiss my mouth, you bite my
lip, you draw blood, you're on fire, you're on fire,
your eyes are flame, your hair is flame, the whole
world shimmers and I burn and I burn with love –

Roxane Christian . . .

Cyrano – the whole world shimmers – and the night –
and the sky – and your voice shimmers – I've no
wit, I've no mind, I've no brake, I've no self-control,
I've no shame, I've no authority over myself, I can
wait hours for just one glimpse of you then not
speak to you at all, how can I speak, how can
I speak to you, I can't speak, I can't stop speaking,
I can't stop looking, I can't look, I make you an
object, I desire you, I write to you, I write for you,
I tear up everything I have ever written for you or
about you, I burn myself alive for you, I worship
you, I strip you, I clothe you, I do up the tiniest
buttons at your sleeve, I embrace your wrist, I embrace
your neck, I kiss the back of your neck, I embrace
your wrist, I'm speechless, speechless, all I can say is
I want – I want – I want – there is no poetry – there
is no structure that can make any sense of this –
only I want – I want – I want – I want you, Roxane.

Pause.

Roxane I want you too. Kiss me.

*Cyrano moves towards her. She's about to turn when
Christian gently moves him out of the way. As Roxane
turns, she sees Christian coming towards her. They
kiss. Cyrano watches this, then turns away in distress.*

Christian and Roxane continue to kiss.

A Priest appears and watches them.

Priest Madeleine Robin?

Cyrano indicates the kissing couple.

                What? With that man?
Excuse me. Excuse me. Madeleine Robin?

She disengages from Christian.

Roxane Yes? Sorry? Can I help you?

Priest   I have a letter
for you.

Roxane   Ah. Okay. Well you'd better
show it me. (*Sees Cyrano.*) Cyrano?
                              I thought you'd gone.

Cyrano Yes – almost –

Roxane   What? – is something wrong?

Cyrano No – not at all – seems there's a priest . . .

Priest Yes I've a letter – it's from the Comte de Guiche.

Roxane
De Guiche? – what's de Guiche got to do with me?

Priest He respects the Church, Mademoiselle:
                    it's sure to be something profound and holy.

Cyrano Can I get you a drink, Father?

*While Cyrano pours himself and the priest a drink,
Roxane opens the letter and reads it under her breath.*

Roxane 'Roxane. I couldn't leave. Have taken the room
I spoke to you about. Be there soon.
One night, Roxane. You won't regret it.
If you want tenderness, you'll get it.
Or you can defy me, Roxane – but if you do
believe me, I can be brutal too.
This priest will do whatever I say.
He's just a jobs-worth in my pay.
He'll assume this is a holy mission:
and bow – as you must –

                         to my status and position.'

Everyone looks at Roxane, who's in a state of shock.

Priest What are the comte's instructions? Mademoiselle?

Roxane What? I'll read them to you. *No, but this is Hell.*

Gathers her strength, and 'reads' from the letter.

'Roxane, the priest who brings this letter
is reverent and wise, I know none better.
I hereby instruct him as a God-fearing man
to join you in marriage to . . . Christian.
Do this immediately. This is the will
not just of me (*Turns page.*) but of the Cardinal.
Do not defy me, Roxane, since if you do
God himself – yes God – God – God will punish you.
Marry Christian. Do it. Do not resist but pray.
It's God's will. Humble yourself, Roxane. Obey.'

Priest
Well, Mademoiselle – my instructions are very clear . . .

Roxane I won't do it! I refuse!

Priest (*meaning Cyrano*)   This gentleman here
is to become your husband.

Cyrano   Me? I don't think so.

Roxane   NO!
This letter forces me to marry *this* one –
                        this revolting man –
this creep – this scumbag Christian.

Priest Scumbag? But weren't the two of you just . . . ?

Roxane What? What? Yes and he kissed me –
                        so? – was that my fault? –
he *forced* himself on me – you saw –
                        did I consent? – no – it was *assault*.

Pause.

Priest Well once you're married it'll be alright:
it won't be assault then, it will be his right.
Inside please. You and the handsome groom.

Just fifteen minutes and a private room –
that's all we need.

Roxane   DON'T TOUCH ME! NO!
(*Sotto.*) Cyrano – please –
if he turns up, can you waylay de Guiche?

Priest Come on now. Don't be afraid. It is God's plan
that woman subjugates herself respectfully to man.

They go into the inner room, leaving Cyrano alone.

Cyrano Waylay de Guiche? So my role
is bare my soul
then crawl back into my lonely language-hole.
Waylay de Guiche. Be decoy.
Play dead. Be voice only of that pretty boy.
Waylay de Guiche. Play my part.
Lay bare my soul – but still obtain

                                no access to her heart.
Waylay de Guiche. Hmm.

Then having to watch them kiss . . .
I'd no idea it could ever feel as bad as this . . .

*He wraps himself up and somehow disguises himself.
De Guiche arrives.*

De Guiche Where the hell's that priest?

Cyrano groans.

De Guiche   What's that? What's going on? Roxane?

Cyrano Help me. Where am I? Are you a man?

De Guiche Are you hurt? What is it you're doing here?

Cyrano Are you a man? Where am I? What is this place?

De Guiche Where've you come from?

Cyrano   Come from? Come from? Space.

De Guiche Space?

Cyrano   I rose up – space, yes – in a red balloon
  and travelled to the dark side of the moon.

De Guiche I'm sure.

Cyrano   But sick of that perpetual night
  crawled my way back through moondust to the light.

De Guiche Glad to hear it. Now cut the bullshit.

Cyrano (*grabs him*)
  No. What place is this? Where did I land?

De Guiche Don't touch me like that. Remove your hand.

Cyrano Must be Earth –

De Guiche   Remove your hand.

Cyrano   – On Earth, you see,
  the inhabitants often behave like this – violently.

  He releases De Guiche. Pause.

De Guiche Look – I have business here –
  out of my way please – disappear.
  And if it's at all possible
  you should make your way back now

                         to the mental hospital.

Cyrano Business?

De Guiche   I'm sorry?

Cyrano   What business is that?

De Guiche I keep my business, thank you, under my hat.

Cyrano Oh? Earth-business. Can we assume
  it's something we don't come across then on the moon?
  Some kind of man-woman thing? Don't be shy.

De Guiche Look. Mind your own business, madman.
                I don't have to tell you why / I'm here.

Cyrano Oh? Then shall I perhaps break both your legs?

Pause. He means it. De Guiche smiles.

De Guiche
Alright – yes – I'm meeting a woman here for sex.
Satisfied?

Cyrano   Yes, yes – very understandable:
you look like a man, but in fact you are an animal.

Pause.

De Guiche Do I know you?

Cyrano   Know me?
Only if you've studied moon-life very closely.

De Guiche Life? There's no life on the moon. Now leave.

Cyrano
No life? – really? – is that seriously what you believe?
Well yes – maybe there is no air –
but all the same there's moon-men everywhere –
the nights are ice
but in the day it's paradise:
trees, flowers, sparkling streams,
are what we see on waking from our dreams.
We drink hot coffee. Then look! – Earth rises! –
a haze of blue masks all its earthly vices –
war – lust – greed – the violence of the crowd –
are hidden by its spiral threads of cloud
and from the moon all that we moon-men see 's
a turning planet with no history.

De Guiche You're mad.

Cyrano   Nobody starves. Women are respected.
Men are not animals. Nobody's infected
with hate – or fear – there are no slaves
or calculated massacres – no shallow graves.

No – seen from the moon the Earth's devoid of vice:
and this of course is why our morning coffee
                              tastes so nice.

De Guiche Well thanks for the adolescent lecture. Now
    if you don't mind
there's a young woman here I really need to find –
I've booked us a room – or that at least
is what I thought I had agreed on with that fucking
    priest.

Cyrano A priest?

De Guiche   Yes. Have you seen him?

Cyrano Seen a priest?

De Guiche   Yes. Or the woman.

Cyrano Seen a woman.

De Guiche   Yes. Time's running out.

Cyrano How old is she?

De Guiche   God knows – must be about
    nineteen? twenty? I spoke to that priest –
                    I BOOKED A ROOM –

Cyrano (*very softly*) Oh by the way:
                    one other thing about the moon . . .

De Guiche
    What? No. No. No, I'm sick of this. Jesus and Moses!

Cyrano (*very softly*) I think I should tell you
                    about the moon-men's noses.

    De Guiche becomes wary.

De Guiche Their noses? Why?

Cyrano   No reason – just we have a lunar rule:
    the measure of a nose becomes the measure of a fool –

by which I mean to caution
you that fool and nose-size are in inverse proportion.

De Guiche I don't quite follow.

Cyrano   We have a formula that goes
'Fool over six is x times square root of Nose.'

De Guiche I don't do maths. Stop this. What d'you mean?

Cyrano It's really quite simple – haven't you been
listening? A moon-man's nose is sacred.
It rises between his eyes, honourable and naked.
The longer it is the more we all respect him.
Since length is a sign of virtue, we protect him
from human mockery. But the small-nosed and weak,
we kill them in the cradle before they can even speak.

De Guiche (*realises*) Cyrano.

Cyrano   Exactly.

Pause. Cyrano casts off his disguise.

De Guiche   Where is Roxane?

Cyrano Well by now she's hopefully married to that man.

De Guiche What man? What're you TALKING ABOUT?

Cyrano They're just behind you. No need to shout.

The others have indeed appeared from the inner room.

De Guiche Married?

Roxane   Yes. Good evening, de Guiche.

De Guiche Don't you good evening me, you bitch.

Priest Monsieur le Comte, she tried to say no
but your letter gave me very clear instructions, so . . .

De Guiche Idiot.

Roxane (*serenely*) Something wrong?
                 We thought this was your plan.

De Guiche Officers – seize this man.

Officers appear.

Roxane What?

De Guiche Oh – oh – didn't you know? –
his regiment was mobilised hours ago.

Christian Mobilised?

Roxane But you said – you promised me no war.

De Guiche Think I'd keep promises, do you, to a whore?

Christian lunges at De Guiche but is restrained.

(*To Christian*) And you. The husband. Leave now
and if not
I'll have you instantly court-martialled here and shot.

Roxane No!

Cyrano Leave him be, Roxane.

Roxane Just one night!

De Guiche
If he's got the energy to fuck he's got the energy to fight.
I said leave.

They start to go.

Roxane (*to Cyrano*) Please keep him safe.

Cyrano I'll try to.

Roxane And make him behave
sensibly.

Cyrano I'll try to.

Roxane I'm scared.

Cyrano He'll be fine.

Roxane I'm just so totally unprepared
for this.

Cyrano He'll be back.

Roxane Tell him to write.
I want really long letters – please? –
really long letters – starting tonight.
Make him. D'you promise? Say: 'Write to Roxane.'

Cyrano Really long letters – I'll do what I can.

Act Four

INTERIOR: A FIREBASE OUTSIDE ARRAS

5.30 a.m. A row of sleeping soldiers.

Le Bret and another man have just come off sentry duty. They speak as quietly as possible.

Man Time?

Le Bret   Zero five thirty.

Man   Reveille?

Le Bret   Yup.
  What?

Man   Can't face waking the poor fuckers up.

Le Bret Do it.

Man   No food – hardly any water –

Le Bret Do it. Five thirty-one – we ought to
  be waking them.

Man   Got any dried fruit?

Le Bret Saving it for Christmas – come on now: do it.

  Pause.

  What?

Man   Dunno. This whole night on stag [*night watch*] –
  feels like I'm going a bit fucking mad –
  you've really got no fruit?

Le Bret   It's getting late –
  why don't we save the whole fruit debate
  till everyone's standing to. Okay?

Man Okay.

Le Bret We've still got water for what? half a day? –
so let's keep calm about this – we'll be fine –
we'll just move very very gently down the line . . .

They head off towards the sleepers.

Man Oh Jesus Christ who the fuck is that!

Le Bret Shit! He was about to kill you, Bergerac!

Cyrano has appeared.

Man Don't do that, man!

Cyrano   Sorry. I've been out.

Le Bret You've been OUT?

Cyrano   Yes – yes – try not to shout –
you know that one of the beauties
of this job is performing my early morning duties –

Le Bret These stupid letters.

Cyrano   I promised he would write
to her. It's not stupid – in fact it's a delight
to crawl each night across no man's land
and deliver each letter into the hand
of my special contact.

Le Bret   Provided you don't get shot.

Cyrano Well, so far I've not.

Pause.

You do know there's a rumour we may re-supply.

—— You serious?

Cyrano (*smiles*)
And another one that we're all of us going to die.
Take your pick.

Le Bret   You're risking your life for nothing.

Cyrano My word is not nothing. I'd rather be suffering
hunger than dishonour.

Man   But what about thirst?
No clean water – dehydration's the worst.
You'd think he could at least fill us a bottle
when he's finished crawling – whatever –

                                    across the rubble.

Cyrano
Fair point – and it's something I would certainly do
if their water – I'm sorry – wasn't poisoned too.

Le Bret It's a mess.

Man   The whole op's gone to rats –
here we are – meant to lay siege to Arras –
but the supply line's cut and we're in more jeopardy
than the fucking enemy.

Le Bret Okay now – easy – come on – get a
grip.

Cyrano moves away.

         Cyrano?

Cyrano   Just need to write one more letter.

He sits apart and writes.

Man Sorry, Le Bret.

Le Bret   No worries.

Man   I thought he
was *them*. [*the enemy*]

Le Bret   Come on. Zero five-forty.

*They start to very gently wake the other men,
whispering 'stand to', 'stand to'.
    Cyrano writes.*

Eventually the other soldiers begin to speak, all very softly.

—— Fucking parrot's cage, mate.

——   I've got some spit.

—— Pass it round then.

——   Fuck you – I'm swallowing it.

They laugh.

—— Cracked lips. Got this kind of crust round my eyes.

—— Sure, lover-boy – told you you should moisturise.

They laugh.

You're not employing enough product.

—— Say product once more and you're fucked.
Hey, Le Bret – what's the allowance? Still rationed?

Le Bret   Yup – forty-five mil.
every two hours.

——   What would you give for rain?

—— Left arm. Left leg. Both ears.

——   Brain.

—— Arsehole.

——   One bollock.

——   Hang on to your dick.

—— Yeah – keep the dick – but the left arm I would stick
in a small wooden box and post it home.

—— (*laughs*) That is morbid.

——   And I'd include a poem.

Pause.

—— (*sotto*) What's up with Jean-Paul?

—— (*sotto*)   Misses his kids –
got three – loves them to fucking bits –

—— (*sotto*) Two boys plus a new daughter –

—— Hey – Le Bret – time to share out that water.

In silent concentration they share out the water –
45 ml. (about two egg-cupfuls) each – and drink it.

—— Cyrano – you're missing out.

Cyrano   Not thirsty – I'm fine.

—— Come on – water.

Cyrano   No – you have mine.

He goes on writing. Pause.

—— What was the name of that book you had?

Cyrano You mean this? Homer – the *Iliad*.

—— What's that all about then?

Cyrano (*sealing his letter*) About a bunch of men –
and they're fighting a war –
and they've kind of forgotten what the war is even for –
but they can't stop. And the war can't end
till Achilles kills Hector to avenge his dead friend
Patroclus.

——   Sounds cheery.

Cyrano   Yes – but possibly
the touchstone for all poetry.

—— You are obsessed.

Cyrano   I love words, that's all.

88

And without this – (*Holds up pen.*)
                    human history would fall
into a black pit
and there'd be almost no trace of it.

Pause.

—— Come on – you need to drink, man.

Cyrano When he wakes up, give it to Christian.

He turns away and leafs through the book.

*The other men start to tap out a rhythm very softly
with their mess-tins – of increasing complexity, never
more than pianissimo. Then softly chant –*

—— Who's the man we always back?

—— Cyrano de Bergerac.

—— Who can take the fucking flak?

—— Cyrano de Bergerac.

—— Who is it the twats attack?

—— Cyrano de Bergerac.

—— Here we go.

—— Cyrano.

—— Our hero.

—— Cyrano.

—— Who would go to hell and back?

—— Cyrano. Cyrano. Cyrano de Bergerac.

—— Who is it reads the *Iliad*?

—— Cyrano. Cyrano. Cyrano de Bergerac.

—— Book attack.

—— Bergerac.

—— White or black.

—— Bergerac.

—— On the rack.

—— Bergerac.

—— Hell and back.

—— Bergerac. Bergerac. Cyrano de Bergerac.

This continues and only stops a little while after De Guiche appears, also suffering from dehydration.

De Guiche Zero six hundred. You may stand down.
You're an excellent team. I'm very proud
of all of you. I still have some difficulty
with the fact that you despise me –
but so be it . . .

He's struggling to ignore the unused ration of water.

I have my pride
and you all know that I have fought vigorously
alongside
you. (*Pause.*) There seems to be an unused ration of . . .

Cyrano   Water. Yes.
We were keeping it to brush our teeth – unless / you . . .

De Guiche No – no – excellent. Waste
not want not. I ate my toothpaste.
But as I was saying – bit of a dry mouth –
we've all seen action – and in fact when I was in south
sector yesterday – well you probably heard
about the fire-fight –

Cyrano   little bird
told me you'd torn off your flash.

De Guiche (*with pride*) Yes, with a certain . . . panache
 I did indeed tear off my identifying material
 to avoid being a target. I was nearly a
 dead man but that little trick saved me.

Cyrano Very good.

De Guiche   Thank you, Cyrano. (*Slight pause.*)
          You've something
           to say to me?

Cyrano No no – just re-reading the *Iliad*,
 that's not an idea a Greek hero would ever've had.

De Guiche Bullshit. The Greeks were all tricky.
          Look at Odysseus.

Cyrano He wasn't trusted. He was the one introduced
 deceit into warfare. Where is the flash now?

De Guiche What? No idea. I really don't see how
 I could answer that question.

Cyrano   I'd've retrieved it.

De Guiche Bullshit, man – you don't really believe that –
 have you seen the south sector? –
        whole area's been strafed –
 there's sniper fire – it's totally unsafe –
 no shade – no cover – the enemy can appear
 without warning . . . What is that?

Cyrano   I have your flash here.

*He holds it up. Appreciative soft clatter of mess-tins
from the others.*

De Guiche Well. Thank you. I shall sew it back on.
 Now. Briefing. Briefing time, gentlemen –
 bit of a dry mouth – it's deep shit, everyone –
 the fact is is what with the issues of supply –

—— We're up a rat's arse and we're all going to die.

Laughter.

De Guiche I wouldn't go quite so far
as to say that – yes we are
challenged – it is 360-degree war –
but the battle group has begun to explore
options. A line has been opened now to the east
for food and water and we've vastly increased
their support. We will soon have the critical mass
of firepower in place to take Arras.
However – protecting that line has drained resources
here, and the enemy knows this.
Intelligence is: they will attack.
This is good: we buy time for the others. What we lack
in numbers we will make up for in ferocity.

Le Bret realises what this means.

Le Bret We block.

De Guiche You block – you use high velocity
weapons – draw fire – I know you cadets
like extreme danger. And it's what France expects.

Pause. Christian speaks for the first time.

Christian You've volunteered us for a suicide mission.

De Guiche Yes – you're dispensable. That's my position.
I can't pretend I'm upset especially –
but trust you won't take it personally.
Besides, there's at least one man here
likes a hundred-to-one odds.
                              Do I make myself clear?

De Guiche looks like he may faint.

Cyrano Give him the water.

De Guiche   No thank you, Cyrano.

Cyrano Drink it.

——   Here, mate – take it.

De Guiche   I TOLD YOU NO.

He knocks the water to the ground. Shocked silence.

Come with me, Le Bret –
I want to discuss the weapon-checks.

They move away.

Cyrano Christian?

Christian   He's losing his mind.

Cyrano   You've slept?

Christian Not a lot. It's the end, then.

Cyrano   What did you expect?

Christian I need to write her a farewell letter.

Cyrano I've done it.

Christian   Show me.

*Cyrano reluctantly produces the letter. Christian takes
it and stares at him.*

Cyrano   What?

Christian   D'you get a
kick out of this?

Cyrano   Kick?

Christian   Sorry – that was hateful –
you've helped me a lot – I'm really really grateful –
but why do you do this, Cyrano?

Cyrano I love you, Christian – and you know
I'd do anything for you and for Roxane.

*Christian glances through the letter without really
reading it.*

Christian Fucking hell!

Cyrano   What?

Christian   This letter is fucking tear-stained, man.

Cyrano How could that be?

Christian   So what's this?

Cyrano   Must be sweat.

Christian I suppose.

Cyrano   You're over-reacting.

Christian   Right.

Cyrano   I've not wept
over anything or anyone for years.
It's sweat, Christian – just looks like tears.

They look at each other.

A shot is heard.

Two figures rush in, pursued by soldiers.

—— Down! Drop your weapons! On the ground!
Show your hands! I said hands!

——   Turn around!
Hands! Fucking hands! Show your face! Face!
It's a bomb! Back! Back! Bastards they're
                      going to detonate!

Le Bret Hold your fire!

*As everyone backs away, the two figures slowly raise
their hands and begin to laugh.*

Roxane   Oh my God – such a fuss!

Leila Go easy, my friends – it's only us –
  what d'you think, Roxane – shall we just go home?

Roxane Not much of a welcome –

Leila   – too much testosterone.

Christian (*almost in tears*) Fucking idiots –
                              you could've been killed.

Roxane Love you too, sweetheart.

Leila   Come on, guys – chill.

De Guiche How did you get here?

Roxane   What? – helpless females?

Leila We just appeared – like they do in fairy-tales.

De Guiche You appeared?

Leila   Well, Roxane went to the ministry
  and kind of –

Roxane   – really bad –

Leila   – deployed her femininity
  to . . .

Roxane   Stole a map. From the most distinguished of
     sources –
  shows the positions of the enemy and of all our armed
     forces.

  Slight pause.

Le Bret It's not funny – you're risking lives –

Roxane Sorry? We thought wives
  and girlfriends were crucial
  to male morale. Or is the army going gender-neutral?
  What does my cousin say? He's unusually quiet.

Cyrano Everyone here is starved, Roxane, and tired, and very pleased to see you –

Roxane   Good.

Cyrano   – amazed
at your survival skills – a little crazed
by thirst – but – um – how can I put this . . .?

Le Bret Bad timing.

Cyrano   Yes.

De Guiche   An operation –

Roxane   Oh?
What does he mean, an operation, Cyrano?

Cyrano To block the enemy.

Leila   To block?

Christian   Means fight –
means fight till no one here is left alive,
Roxane. Those are our instructions.

Roxane   Instructions from who?

De Guiche From the commanding officer.

Roxane   You?

De Guiche That's right.

Roxane absorbs this.

Roxane   You piece of shit.

Cyrano   Back off, Roxane.

Roxane Back off? Fuck you. He wants to kill my husband.

Leila Calm down, girl.

Roxane   Don't you calm down girl me –
you fucking piece of shit, de Guiche –

please somebody help me –
instructions? – I'LL RIP HIS TONGUE OUT.

She launches herself at De Guiche and starts
pummelling him with her fists. The others pull her
away, and she ends up being gently held by Christian.

De Guiche   Access should be denied.
I'll speak to the sentry – find out
how these two women got inside.

De Guiche goes out.

Roxane
Well . . . sorry about the scene. Who'd like a drink?
Gin? Whisky? What d'you think?

Cyrano There's nothing here, Roxane.

Christian   Not even water.

Roxane
No? Oh what a shame. Here's us and we've brought a
whole load of snacks. Haven't we, Leila.
No water? – sounds like a manly logistical failure.

Leila Yes, and some condoms too.

Cyrano   Condoms.

Christian   They're mad.

Roxane Really? We were told you quick wits
in the army use them to carry liquids.

She and Leila open their coats to show they have
supplies strapped to their bodies, including water-filled
condoms.

—— Oh my God – water.

——   Water and food.

——   Fucking genius.

Leila So – precious friends – be less abstemious
   eat – drink – be joyful – take heart –

—— What's this?

Leila   That, boy, is a traditional French lemon tart –

—— Amazing.

Leila   Twelve ounces of refined
   sugar, juice of four lemons plus their grated rind.
   Quintessence of French patisserie
   and rich enabler –

—— (*several*)   OF POETRY.

Leila (*softly*)   – of poetry.

Everyone starts to concentrate on eating and drinking.

—— Cut it open, man – what're you waiting for?

—— Don't tell me you've never split a condom before.

—— Pass that pastry.

Cyrano (*sotto*)   Christian – Christian, can we talk?

—— That is sweet.

——   A culinary work
   of art, Madame Ragueneau.

Cyrano (*sotto*)   Christian –

Roxane No you don't, Cyrano. I want this man
   of mine all to myself. Your poor lips
   are all cracked. Does it hurt to kiss?

—— (*mock disgust*)   Leave it out.

——   Trying to eat.

Christian pulls back.

Roxane   Christian, what's wrong?

Christian Nothing.

—————   Hey, Leila, do us a poem.

—————   Yeah: poem, come on.

LEILA'S POEM

Because I could not stop for death
he kindly stopped for me
I asked to see a photograph
confirming his identity.

The faces matched – the eyes were warm –
the hair was long and grey –
both smiled but as I tried to move
death blocked my way.

No no, my sweetheart, what's the rush?
Come on, let's go to bed,
there's time for love, there's surely time
for happiness – death said.

His voice was soft, his skin was pale,
his fingers brushed my face –
Oh? time for love? I said – but where?
He said: I know a place.

He led me down a flowered track
and on a bank of earth
he loved me till my body screamed
from every living nerve.

I slept then for eternity
drugged as I was with love:
death bent down to my sleeping face
and on earth's pillow made a space
to leave his photograph.

Applause.

*During the poem De Guiche has appeared. He is
confused to see everyone eating and drinking.*

De Guiche Food. Must be hallucinating.
  Is that really food you're eating?

Leila There's water too.

Le Bret   Come on, de Guiche – drink some.

De Guiche This isn't real. I think some
  thing's happening to my mind. What's that?

Cyrano Water, de Guiche.

De Guiche   I owe you all an apology.
  I've behaved insensitively.
  I . . .

—— Give him a drink.

De Guiche   . . . I've decided
  to stay with you and fight alongside
  you.

—— Bravo!

De Guiche   To the death.

Cyrano   Let's hope not.

Le Bret Come on – drink the water.

De Guiche   I've spoken a lot
  of bullshit. I'm ashamed.

  *He drinks water for a long time. Everyone watches in
  silence.*

Christian (*to Roxane*) You should go back.

Roxane Go back? How?

De Guiche   It's too late for that.
  Ladies, we need to find you a place of safety.

Leila Aren't we safe here?

De Guiche   This building's a target. Maybe
  – gentlemen? – you could help me find

them a safe location. Would you mind?

Everyone starts to go out . . .

Roxane What does he mean?

—————   There are tunnels, love,
underground.

Leila In the dark?

—————   Less risk of you being found.

Le Bret Move please. There's not much time.

Leaving Christian and Cyrano alone.

Christian   Talk? What did you mean?

Cyrano About the letters.

Christian   What about them?

Cyrano If they're discussed. If you and she . . .

Christian I do know who wrote them. I know it's not me.

Cyrano Yes but there's one more thing –

Christian   What thing is that?

Cyrano The frequency – because in fact
there are more letters than you think.

Christian   Meaning what?

Cyrano Meaning more – meaning many – meaning not
simply one each week.

Christian   But you agreed –

Cyrano I agreed – yes – but then I got this kind of need
to go on writing.

Pause.

                   Don't look at me like that.

Christian How many, Cyrano?

Cyrano   Well. Quite a stack.

Christian
  Two a week? Three? Three a week? Come on. Say.

Cyrano More than that. Maybe two letters a day?

Christian Two a day?

Cyrano   Yes.

Christian   And you've risked your own life

Cyrano yes

Christian   to deliver

Cyrano   I know

Christian   all these letters

Cyrano   you're right

Christian   to MY WIFE?

  Pause.

Cyrano I can't stop myself.

Christian   But Cyrano, don't you see:
  you are not her husband. YOU ARE NOT ME.

Cyrano Keep your voice down – she's coming.

Christian   You're insane.

Cyrano Well, yes, maybe – maybe it does have a name –
  maybe it is madness – the madness of a poem / or . . .

Roxane Cyrano – I think Christian and me would like
    to be alone
  now.

Cyrano Of course.

Cyrano goes.

Roxane　　　　　Is he okay? He looks so intense.

Christian　You know what he's like. Thinks the whole
　　world's against
him and so on.

Roxane　　　　　Which it probably is.

Christian　Yes.

Takes her hand.

Roxane　　　　What?

Christian　　　　　　I'm not sure about this,
　　Roxane – this visit's extremely dangerous –

Roxane　Oh no – there are these tunnels –
　　　　　　　　le Bret has just / explained to us –

Christian　Why did you come?

Roxane　　　　　　　　　To see you – to bring food.

Christian　Yes, but why?

Roxane　　　　　　Don't talk to me like that.

Christian　　　　　　　　　　　　Good –
　　yes – sorry – food – but it is extreme
to come here now.

Roxane　　　　　Well maybe extreme's my dream.
　　You yourself write about love's limits –
that there are none – that love is a Phoenix
and the more intense the fire
and the brighter love burns, the higher
we can fly.

Christian　　I myself write.

Roxane　　　　　　　　Well yes!

I despise the sentimental but the fact is, Christian,
   is this:
your writing's changed me. I was quite precious.
But since you started writing all these amazing letters
I'm not the same. Plus I can
see inside you – not just the surface –
               but right through you to the man.
You ask why I've come – well might not the
most honest answer be: to meet the writer?

Christian Meet the writer.

Roxane   Come on – it's like what you said:
how we would dream the same dreams
                  together in the same bed.

Christian I wrote that?

Roxane   Yes – yes in the letter where
you cry as you are pushing your fingers through my hair.
You've not forgotten?

Slight pause.

Christian   Roxane –

Roxane   Plus I've also
started to think about beauty – it's all so . . .
fucking relative . . .

*Not touching her, but trying to close down the
conversation.*

Christian   Roxane, not now –

Roxane   Hey, stop that –
I'm trying to talk. And it's not that
there isn't beauty in the world: there is –
but beauty evolves – that's one of its mysteries.
No – hear me out. And God when I think how inflamed
I was by your physical appearance I'm actually ashamed.

Christian Ashamed?

Roxane Well yes of course: it's skin –

Christian Ashamed?

Roxane – it's just – yes – this envelope
the actual person's hidden in –
I know this from your letters: *that* is what's real –
the thing inside – not just what? – 'sex-appeal' –
or being 'hot' or 'fit' or 'fuckable'
and all these horrid ways we label people –
no. And I admit it. There
was a time I thought it mattered. Now I don't care.

Christian Roxane?

Roxane I don't. You could be –
whatever – shit-looking – poor –
I'd still want you. I'd want you more.

Pause.

Who's that?

A soldier is trying to get her attention.

Christian Go with him.

Roxane The guy in pyjamas? [*combats*]
What's that he's holding?

Christian For you – please go – it's body-armour.

Roxane goes to put on the body-armour.

*Christian suppresses his rage before kicking something
over – or some other violent act.*

Cyrano appears.

(*Sotto.*) Oh fuck you, Cyrano.

Cyrano What? What has she said?

Christian Dream the same dream in the same fucking bed.

Cyrano It's your love-letter.

Christian   It's a letter from *you*.
It's from *you*. I'm not anything to *do*
with this. Am I? Am I?
I'm just – what – the regular army guy –
Mister Provincial Nobody plodding along
while this whole other love story's going on –

Cyrano I'm sorry –

Christian   No you're not.
You love her – you want her –
                              now that's what you've got.
Shit-looking.

Cyrano   Christian.

Christian   Shit-looking. All this *reading*
she's done – this 'beauty evolves' – this needing
to quote your letters – this 'I don't care
what a man looks like'? Really? But of course that
    is where
you score so highly – the man with the nose.
And the acres of highbrow wet-dream prose.

Pause.

Cyrano Wet-dream prose – that's not bad.

Christian   Yes and
I can do without the fucking writing lesson.

Both laugh a little, but tension remains.
    Pause.

Cyrano I think you're over-reacting. What I wrote
has meant something to her – great – she can quote
it – okay.
But that does not mean to say

she would go with a shit-looking man.
She may say it – but come on, Christian –
you're her husband. Her reaction
to you 's one of pure non-negotiable sexual attraction.

Slight pause.

What?

Christian I don't know. Is there a version
of life where two men can live as one person?

*Christian kisses Cyrano – tentatively at first, but with
increasing intensity. Then backs away.*

No . . . No . . .

Cyrano   Christian.

Christian   No.

Christian starts to leave, as Roxane appears.

Cyrano   Christian!

Roxane   What's happening?

Christian (*as he goes*) Cyrano has something important
                              to say to you.

Cyrano Christian, come back!

Roxane   Why's he running?

Cyrano (*grabs her*)   Don't.
  Don't follow him.

Roxane   That hurts. Get off of me. I want
  to know what's happening.

Cyrano   Just the letters. He's upset.

Roxane What about? That hurts!

Cyrano   The thing, Roxane, the thing you said
  about ugly.

Roxane   About ugly?

Cyrano   Beauty – does it exist? –
  does it matter? –

Roxane   You're breaking my wrist.

Cyrano   – what counts? – would you be satisfied
  if a man was beautiful only on the inside?

Roxane What? YES. YES.

Cyrano   So the real Christian
  is the one in the letters?

Roxane   Yes of course. Can
  I go now? Of course he is *real* –
  he's my husband – I love him – what is the deal
  with this interrogation? – GET OFF! –

Gunfire. He releases her.

                                    What is that?

Cyrano Enemy fire. They've started the attack.

Roxane Where's Christian?

Cyrano   You should leave here now.

Roxane Where is Leila?

Cyrano   Somebody showed you how
  to get into the tunnel – yes?

Roxane   Where is she?

Cyrano She will be fine. Just –

*Gunfire intensifies – Le Bret appears with other
soldiers.*

Le Bret   Enemy
  fire – get her the fuck out, Bergerac.

Cyrano I'm trying.

Le Bret   Try harder.

Men rush in with a figure on a stretcher.

——   Wounded soldier!

—   Where's that medic?

—   Mind your back!

—— Stay with us!

——   Any pulse? – well?

——   Not so good.

—— Pressure on the chest, please.

——   We're losing blood.

Le Bret Cyrano, this will be a fucking rout –
I need you in position and GET THAT CIVILIAN OUT!

—— (*of the wounded man*) No heart-beat.

——   Pressure on the chest please – go go go!.

—— Oh fuck it.

Roxane (*with growing horror*) Who's that man, Cyrano?

Cyrano Come on – out.

Roxane   Is he dead?

——   INCOMING MORTAR
TWO O'CLOCK TAKE COVER.

Explosion.

Cyrano   Thank you for the water
but now come on.

Roxane   Is he dead?

Cyrano   Just keep back –

Roxane Don't tell me what to do, Cyrano de Bergerac! –
let me go!

Cyrano   Don't look. It's no one. Just a man.

He drags her away.

You'll do what you're told now.

Roxane   Christian! Christian!

The sound of the battle intensifies.

Act Five

Fifteen years later. Early morning.

Leila – Madame Ragueneau – is knitting in silence.
Lignière watches.

Lignière Didn't know you did knitting.

Pause.

Got no classes?

Pause.

Coffee, Lignière?

Pause.

Thank you. Don't mind if I do.

He operates the machine and makes himself coffee.
As he does so:

Give me some steam on the coffee machine
is it a sin to grind the bean
hey I begin to mind you being so mean
to me Leila when you are the queen
of the stainless coffee station
mistress of versification
painless teacher of the mystification / of –

Leila (*softly*) Enough, Lignière.

Pause.

Lignière Then say what's happened to your classes –
the poetry girls – the chat –
            the young ones with the red-hot asses –

Leila I said enough. You talk that sex shit
like you were nineteen years old still.
Show some respect.
And there are no classes because
the world has changed. Those
in the know speak only –

Lignière   prose?
I do not believe it.

Leila   Well, it's God's truth.
Rhyming is dead –

Lignière   – then show me proof.

He's caught her out. Both laugh a little.

Corneille's still writing – there's Racine . . .

Leila (*not listening*) Plus the French elite
are anti-sugar now – rots their white teeth.
My business is dying.

Lignière . . . you've got la Fontaine – this new guy
Molière – he's copied stuff from Cyrano – it's really
funny – acts in his own plays – he's making so much
money and the whole thing's verse.

Leila It's ending, Lignière. You are behind the wave.
Prose is coming, and it's going to bulldoze away
everything we know. There's going to be a new force in
words – a new resource – no rules – freedom – I will
be dead, but I feel it coming.

Slight pause.

What?

Lignière (*sotto*) What is she doing back there?

Leila Who?

Lignière She's sitting in the back there reading.

Leila She does that. She just comes in. I give her coffee.

Lignière I understand she likes it with a bit of brandy.

Leila That's her business.

Roxane appears.

Lignière (*greeting*) Hey! Roxane!

Roxane Lignière.

They embrace.

Lignière Never thought I'd see this woman knitting.

Leila And why not?

Lignière How go the studies?

Roxane Sorry? – the what?

Lignière The studies – first girl at the University –

Roxane What does he mean?

Lignière Get your degree?

Roxane What?

Lignière The studies – literature – you were so . . .

Leila Lignière, we're talking fifteen years ago.

Roxane sips her coffee.

Roxane I do like books.

Lignière Okay.

Roxane I'm getting into fiction. (*Shows book.*)

Lignière *Princess of . . . Cleves*? What's that?

Roxane I told you – fiction. And from the woman's point of view – they even think a woman wrote it –

Lignière 'Fiction'. Weird.

Roxane Yep – got it from Cyrano –
comes here to see me every day, you know –
lends me books and shit –
tells me about the latest plays –
totally broke –
was homeless for a while after he got back.
But now he's okay –
still got that fire of his –
likes to make enemies –
but such a decent man –
helped me so much –
because when I think about . . .
think about what happened to Christian . . .

Pause.

Leila (*to comfort*) Come on, girl –

Roxane No, don't – no sympathy –
I'm over that –
got my own life now –
got my own flat . . . I . . .

Pause.

Yeah, you should visit:
just off the rue de Rennes – Antoine pays for it –
I don't mean sex –
not really – no –
just wants to watch me . . .
watch me do stuff . . . . . .
Whatever. Do stuff.
So.

Slight pause.

Indicates book.

You can read it if you want.

Lignière Antoine?

Roxane Antoine de Guiche
and don't you start preaching
at me too.
Are you a woman? No. What would you do?
You won't find me sitting
like Leila here doing the fucking knitting.

Pause. She sips her coffee.

Where's Cyrano? He's never late.
Not once. Not ever.
Think I'll just go back inside with this [*book*] and wait.

She goes.

Lignière (*sotto*) She doesn't know?

Leila (*sotto*) Know what?

Lignière About what's happened to Cyrano.

Leila Happened?

Lignière Yes – in the night –
there was this fist-fight
outside the theatre
some writer dear to
the establishment smeared
Roxane
like this man
said she'd disappeared
come back weird
and was turning trash
turning tricks (said this guy) for cash.
Cyrano heard
this and he went berserk

slapped the guy so hard
broke his jaw if not more then started
to lay into his friends.
Next thing you know the ends
of the street get sealed off
he's trapped and there's enough
of them to do some damage.
Still no man can manage
to master Cyrano
he can move faster – blow after blow
watch the man mow
them all down like death.

Slight pause.

But some guy plays low
what's this in his hand
it's a fist – it's a fistful of sand
and he throws it
goes like an explosive
into Cyrano's eyes.
So the man is blind now
and he howls and he's out of his mind now
with rage when they come from behind
and they stick in the knife.
Sure maybe not deep
but he's down on the ground on the sealed-off street
and he's losing blood
and they say could've lost it all
but they scraped him up
and they stretchered him in to the hospital.

Slight pause.

Leila Why didn't you tell me this straight away?

Lignière Thought everyone knew.

Leila picks up her things.

Leila You're making coffee while your friend is dying?

Lignière It's a flesh-wound, Leila.
  The man is fine – just lying
  there in the hospital –
  got the fit nurses – got the fruit –

Leila You come with me, please.

Lignière   Now?

Leila   Just do it.

Lignière The girl?

Leila   She doesn't need to know.
  This way. Not the street. Go go go.

They leave rapidly.

Time passes and Roxane appears.

Roxane Leila? Leila? Top up my coffee?

*The absence of Leila doesn't especially concern her.
She spends a while searching cupboards, eventually
finds the bottle she's looking for and pours a little
alcohol into her coffee cup.
  She doesn't see Cyrano, who is watching her.*

Cyrano Looks like a good idea.

Roxane (*happy*) You scared me. And you're late, Mister
Punctuality. First time ever. Drink?

Cyrano Please.

Roxane   Not too early?

Cyrano   What do you think?

*She pours him a drink. They clink glass and coffee-
cup.*

Roxane So. What kept you?

Cyrano Could I possibly have a chair?

Roxane
I think so. Why not? Chair – chair – just sit anywhere.

He sits.

Where've you been?

Cyrano Went to see a play.

Roxane Oh no. Was it awful?

Cyrano It was brilliant. Full of insight.
Lay awake thinking about it the whole night.

Roxane (*smiles*) You are so obviously lying.

Cyrano Me?

Roxane I know you too well.

Cyrano Oh?

Roxane What's the real reason?

Cyrano Would I lie to you?

Roxane Yes I think that you would. I think that is
something you would definitely do.

Pause.

(*Laughs.*) Your face.

Cyrano What about it?

Roxane (*teasing*)
I think you've been with another woman.

Cyrano A woman?

Roxane Yes. Yes yes yes yes.
I think she came up to you after this play and you've
been fucking all night and most of the morning – why
else the delay?

Slight pause.

Cyrano You're right.

Roxane I knew it.

Cyrano Threw herself at me.

Roxane Of course.

Cyrano Great sex.

Roxane All night long.

Cyrano It's what France expects.

Roxane I can see it.

Cyrano See what?

Roxane You've changed.

Cyrano I'm sorry?

Roxane Changed – yes – yes – what did she do?

Cyrano Changed how?

Roxane Let me see – (*Scrutinising him.*) – hmm – pale – misty-eyed – she really got to you.

Pause.

Cyrano
Listen, I've brought you a few more books, Roxane.

Roxane
You do know me and Christian never slept together?

Cyrano This is the new la Fontaine –

Roxane
It's not nice to be separated on your wedding night –

Cyrano – it's been banned, but I got you a copy –

Roxane – sure it was fifteen years ago and I've still got the letters and of course I've had plenty of other men since but it's weird me and him never actually fucked.

She takes the books.

Oh this one looks cool – *My Life on the Moon* – who's it by? – Cyrano! – it's by you! I'm going to give you a big kiss. Okay, okay – no kissing, but you can at least write in it. Come on: write your name. 'From Cyrano to Roxane'. I'll find a pen.

Cyrano Christian was a boy.

Roxane He was what? Where's a pen?

Cyrano Just a boy. He was confused.

Roxane Oh? Complicated – sure – but confused – never. He put things so clearly in every gorgeous letter he ever wrote. Okay, in the flesh he could be a bit cold. But you're right: he was a boy – and we're both old. Come on now – sign it – 'Cyrano de Bergerac, my journey to the moon and back.'
Oh my God! It's prose!
Is it fiction?

Cyrano Well – the moon . . .

Roxane   Okay – fiction, I suppose.
So impressed! Another drink?

Cyrano   Sure.

Roxane To the author.

Cyrano   *Cincin.*

Roxane   What else is coffee for?

Pause.

Cyrano Roxane?

Roxane Mmm?

Cyrano You still keep the letters?

Roxane Yes.

Cyrano Why's that?

Roxane Why?

Cyrano Yes.

Roxane (*still with humour*) Fuck off.

Cyrano Just all this time –

Roxane Fuck off. The letters are mine.

Cyrano May I see?

Roxane No. Yes. Maybe. Why?

Cyrano No reason – just I . . .

Roxane You what?

Cyrano I'm curious.

Roxane Curious? You're curious? Christian is dead.

Cyrano I know that.

Roxane He died, Cyrano.

Cyrano Of course, but I'd still like to see –

Roxane See what? You think I have the letters with me?

Pause.

Cyrano Do you?

Roxane The last one – yes.
God this place is such a mess now – nobody comes –
but she never asks for money.

Cyrano You have the last letter.

Roxane Yep. Is that horribly sentimental? But there's
something weird about it – cryptic – while the other
ones are all gentle and loving and really quite funny –
but there's this thing he says about lying. Strange.

She's now holding the letter.

Cyrano May I?

She passes it to him.

Roxane Are you alright?

Cyrano I'm sorry?

Roxane Your face – it's . . .

Cyrano It's the light.
Can I read it?

Roxane If you like. Well don't stare at me like that, read
it, it's not going to bite.

Cyrano Roxane –

Roxane Yes?

Cyrano I know what this letter says.

Slight pause.

Roxane Without reading it? Now that is / impressive.

Cyrano Don't hate me.

Roxane Hate you? Why?

Cyrano For what I'm going to tell you.

Roxane (*still thinks it's a game*) Oh oh – mystery man –
so serious! – he 'knows what the letter says' – has
special powers – he / can see through walls –

Cyrano (*simply*) I know what the letters say, Roxane,
because I wrote them all.

Pause.

Roxane Well, I'm used now to men's mad fantasies but this is a new one. No, Cyrano, no – you did not 'write the letters' – what d'you mean? – don't just stare / at me like that –

Cyrano (*holding up the letter, toneless throughout*) 'We've got no water – but can't not fight – so these may be the last words, my sweetheart, I'll ever write.

Slight pause.

'Sweetheart. Is that true? Are you my sweetheart or are you – like I am – one half of a fiction too? Each word I write to you is meant. I love you. Love you so much. But each letter sent also contains a lie – which is hard for a truthful person. So perhaps it is best we die.'

Pause. She realises.

Roxane Give that to me.

Cyrano What?

Roxane Give me that letter now!

Cyrano Roxane.

Roxane And he *made* you do this? –
                          made you write to me? – why? –

Cyrano Don't do that / to the letter.

Roxane   One incredible lie
are you saying, manufactured by two men? –

Cyrano Don't do that / to the letter.

Roxane   Why? Why? How could you agree
to do something so humiliating to me?

Cyrano Please don't do that / to the letter.

Roxane   And how
could you wait all these years only to tell me *now*?

I'll do what I like with the letter.

Cyrano Please. It was not Christian's idea. It was mine.
I wanted to write to you – I forced him to accept –
I was in love with you – I couldn't think of any way
to say it except . . .

Roxane Except?

Cyrano Look   look   look – it wasn't him –
                                    I take all the blame –

Roxane You're telling me you loved me
                                    but you SIGNED HIS NAME –
HIS NAME, Cyrano – how many times? –
a hundred? – more? –
                        what was going on in your mind? –

Cyrano I couldn't . . . [*admit I loved you*]

Roxane And now I'm thinking about that evening –
                        and Christian's voice – that kiss –
the 'tiny buttons' on my sleeve . . .
(*Matter of fact.*) Know what, Cyrano – I'm angry –
and I am burning this.

*The letter burns as he looks on helplessly, now running
out of energy.*

Why could you not just say it?
            I mean what kind of man / is so afraid, he . . .

Cyrano (*simply*) No woman ever looked at me, Roxane.

The letter is burned up.

My role has always been
to play – just as you first asked – the go-between.

Pause.

Roxane Well.
What now?

Your book's out.
Fantastic.
It will be all over the press.
Wonderful.
Will be quite provocative, I guess?
But . . .

. . .

What is it you're really saying to me?
Cyrano?
Seriously.
This trip to the moon.
Instead of fighting are we now taking it together?
Are you inviting me?

Pause.

Cyrano To the moon?

Roxane Because if you want me to, I'll come.

De Guiche Roxane? – Cyrano? – everyone's
been looking for you. Is he alright?

*Lignière and Leila have returned with De Guiche,
whose expensive clothes can't quite compensate for his
physical decline.*

Leila Cyrano – what're you doing here?

Cyrano   Night
was over. I got out of bed.

Lignière That's not what the nurses said –
you are a sick man, Cyrano.

De Guiche Roxane, come here please. We should go.

Roxane What's happening?

De Guiche   He was responsible
for a fight. He's been in hospital.

Roxane No. That's not true.
Cyrano? Tell them.

De Guiche   Have you been drinking?

Roxane   Fuck you.
Tell them, Cyrano. About the book.
He's fine. He was at the theatre.

Leila   Look
at his face, sweetheart. Half blinded him then used
    a knife.
I'm sorry but I've
come here to take him back.

De Guiche   And please:
let me take care of any unwelcome medical fees.

Leila Appreciated.

Roxane   No.

Leila   Help me, Lignière.
Get him on to his feet.

Roxane   You leave him where
he is – you're going to kill him, Leila.

De Guiche Get him out of here –

Lignière   Shit he's getting paler
and paler –

Leila   Can you stand up? Give me your hand . . .

Roxane Don't touch him.

Cyrano (*smiling*)   Well, of course I can stand.

*Cyrano rises magisterially to his feet. The others back
away. Not immediately noticeable is a dark, distinct
bloodstain below his ribs.*

Lignière, Leila, Monsieur de Guiche
– heartbroken and breaking Roxane – to each
of you I am going
to dedicate now my final poem.
Since there is little time I think left to me
I will eschew my usual virtuosity
and be extremely free.
Bear with me.

He summons his strength.

(*Fast and bright.*) Man walks into a bar says
one of those – one of those what?
says the barman quite some nose
you've got there would it like a drink?
– my nose? says the man
well what do you think?
– whisky? says the barman I don't want
no trouble
– whisky says the man and my nose
has a double.

Pause. Cyrano goes blank and sways a little, recovers.
Fast and bright:

Man walks into a bar
says I want to be free
– sure says the barman you can rely on me
what strength freedom
are you looking for
I've got forty per cent sir maybe more
if you can pay for it
up to fifty depends
who's buying have you got rich friends?
– Just free says the man
one hundred per cent
– don't stock it the barman goes
dangerous stuff

makes you puke and see double
freedom that strong
is guaranteed trouble.

Roxane Please stop.

Pause. Cyrano goes blank and sways a little, recovers less successfully.

Cyrano, please stop.

Cyrano (*fast and bright*) Man walks into a bar –

Pause.

Man walks into a bar says
there's this girl outside and
she loves two men
one's really good-looking
the other one all he's got is a pen
so he writes stuff down
and he makes stuff rhyme
does the girl want ice
and a slice of lime
not sure what she drinks
but I think she's trouble –

Pause.

– two men? says the barman
then buy her a double.

Pause.

(*Going blank.*) . . . then buy her a double . . .
Well, my friends – what d'you think of that?

De Guiche (*low and intense to Roxane*)
In fifteen minutes I expect to see you back at the flat.

He leaves.

Lignière It's good – nice rhythm.

Leila   You're on good form.

Cyrano I could make rhymes – and fight –
                                before this man was even born.

Leila The double thing's good.

Lignière   Got real panache –
we loved it.

Cyrano   So why does my life taste like ash?

Slight pause.

(*Smiles.*) Made her so angry!

Roxane   Don't say that – no –
I asked you to help me –

Lignière   Man's a hero.

Roxane – so you did – you meant well. But to be double
is cruel . . .
(*For herself.*) Have I loved two men? – or no men at all?

Cyrano is unsteady.

Someone please help him.

Leila   Hold his hand.

Cyrano   Mouth's gone dry.
Is this how it happens? Is this how I . . . ?

They help him sit in the chair.

(*Smiles.*) Know something? – it was *me* was dreaming –
She was the one used to run round the garden
                                                screaming
and waving that stick –

Pain cuts him off.

Leila Hush now – try not to speak.

Cyrano

Not to speak? Not to speak? But have you not heard? –
the hero always has to have the final . . .

have the final . . . have the . . .

Lights dim.

The hero always has to have the final . . .